A Treatise on Angel Magic

A Treatise on Angel Magic

MAGNUM OPUS HERMETIC SOURCEWORKS

Edited by
Adam McLean

WEISER BOOKS
San Francisco, CA / Newburyport, MA

Published in 2006 by Weiser Books,
an imprint of Red Wheel/Weiser, LLC
York Beach, ME
With offices at:
500 Third Street, Suite 230
San Francisco, CA 94107
www.redwheelweiser.com

Library of Congress has cataloged the previous
edition as follows: 89-29645

Typeset in Garamond

Printed in Canada
TCP

10 9 8 7 6 5 4 3 2 1

The paper used in this publication meets the minimum requirements of
the American National Standard for Information Sciences—Permanence
of Paper for Printed Library Materials Z39.48-1992 (R1997).

Contents

Introduction

Among the Harley collection of manuscripts in the British Library are six volumes written at the end of the seventeenth century which should be of great interest to students of Hermeticism, but which have not yet received much attention. These can be collectively described as 'The Treatises of Dr. Rudd' and they comprise Mss Harley 6481-6486. They seem not to be originals but rather are copies made by a certain Peter Smart in the period 1699-1714.

These documents are of value in that they are compilations of esoteric material from the early seventeenth century, particularly from the Rosicrucian period. At the least, the existence of these manuscripts shows a continuing exploration of the Hermetic tradition into the early eighteenth century.

The manuscripts range over magical, alchemical and Rosicrucian material. We can summarize their contents as follows:

Ms6481   This is described in the Harley Catalogue as follows—
"A quarto containing Dr. Rudd's Treatise of the miraculous Descensions and Ascensions of Spirits, verified by a practical examination of the principles in the Great World—the second part professes to contain some choice Rosicrucian Chymical medicines, wholesome and fit to keep the body in health and lustiness, until the appointed time of death, that is when the soul separates from it. And then teaches the harmony and composition of the human soul, and then conducts it to the source from whence it came. This and the following volumes to 6486 are full of mystical reveries."

Ms6482   *A Treatise on Angel Magic*

Ms6483   "A quarto, containing all the Names, Orders, and Offices of all the Spirits Salomon ever conversed with: the Seals and Characters belonging to each Spirit: and the manner of calling them forth to visible appearance. Some of these Spirits are in Enoch's Tables described in the former volume, but their Seals and Characters, how they may be known are omitted, which are therefore in this book at large set forth."

Ms6484   Dr. Rudd's *Treatise of the Talismanical Sculpture of the Persians, or the manner of making Images under certain constellations*

Ms6485   Primarily an Alchemical compendium comprising three longish texts:
The Rosie Crucian Secrets
A Dictionary of Alchemical term
A Translation of Michael Maier's "Of the Laws and the Mysteries of the Rosicrucians"
(Although 'Rosicrucians' are mentioned in the text of "The Rosie Crucian Secrets" this is primarily a philosophical-practical work on alchemy. At the top of every fourth or fifth folio is the note "the first (etc) sheet of Dr. Dee" indicating perhaps that this item has been copied from a larger manuscript that the author understood to have belonged to Dr. Dee. It is, however, most unlikely that this work was written by John Dee.)

Ms6486   An exact copy of "The Chymical Wedding of Christian Rosenkreutz," claiming to be "translated from the original Latin by Peter Smart, Master of Arts, 1714." However, it is nothing other than a copy of the Ezechiel Foxcroft English translation published in 1690. Smart claims or deludes himself to be copying from an ancient manuscript with marginal notes by Dr. Rudd. These marginal notes are in fact from the printed edition of the work.

Frances Yates examines this manuscript in her *Rosicrucian Enlightenment*, chapter 14. Although recognizing it as a copy of the

Foxcroft translation, she finds it interesting that Peter Smart thought himself to be copying a work which stemmed from John Dee, and he especially emphasises the 'Hieroglyphic Monad' symbol which appears in the margin of the Foxcroft edition (the First Day).

Frances Yates further suggests that the 'Dr. Rudd' was Thomas Rudd, who published an edition of John Dee's *Mathematical Preface* to Euclid in 1651. The Treatise contains a reference to Selden (1584-1654), a renowned antiquary and oriental scholar, confirming that the treatise would have been written down in the middle of the seventeenth century at the earliest. It seems likely that Rudd was heir to esoteric material from the late sixteenth century (period of John Dee) and the early decades of the seventeenth century (the Rosicrucian period); one can thus speculate that he might have been in the circles of Arthur Dee, John Dee's son, who worked in a more alchemical direction than his father, and continued his esoteric studies well into the seventeenth century.

Two other items in the Harley Collection show Rudd to have been a Hebrew scholar sympathetically inclined toward the Jews. Ms6480 is a Hebrew grammar by Rudd, while 6479 is described in the catalogue as "a quarto, containing a defense of the Jews and other Eastern Men, where it is proved that many things are falsely imposed upon the Jews and the rest of the Eastern Men that never were..."

The Treatise on Angel Magic is a compendium of western occult traditions about Angels and related spirits. Dr. Rudd has gathered material from a broad spectrum of primary sources available to him. We can identify some of these quite easily as:

The Three Books of Occult Philosophy of Henry Cornelius Agrippa,

The Lemegeton or *Lesser Key of Solomon,*

Reginald Scott's book on Witchcraft,

Malleus Malleficarum, and

The Arbatel of Magic.

Rudd also seems to have had available a secret tradition about the Enochian Tables of John Dee, which he reveals in a section entitled 'Clavis Enochiani,' the Key of the Tables. This is one of the most important items in this compendium, for it gives us an insight into the use of these seven squares, corresponding to the seven planets, and identifies some of the beings and symbolism associated with these enigmatic magic squares. Although Rudd does not provide an exhaustive account of this system, I believe that with the hints he has here given, it would be possible for an experienced occult scholar and practitioner to work out the full system underlying these squares, and the master diagram within which they are integrated.

The second main section of the work is Dr. Rudd's "Nine Hyerarchies of Angels and their Conjuration to Visible Appearance." This is a most interesting item, for here Rudd reveals himself as a practicing magician, rather than merely a collector or scholar of esoteric material.

He reveals in the structuring of his conjurations an almost obsessive concern with identifying the invoked spirit as a 'good' Angel. There is a hint of paranoiac insecurity about getting in touch with an 'evil' spirit. Consequently, his conjurations are hedged around with tests to trap and make an 'evil' spirit reveal its true colors. Rudd reveals himself here as being immersed in a dualistic picture of the spiritual world. This dualism also shows itself in other sections of his manuscript, particularly in the sections on Demons or Witches and Enchanters, and the fact that he sets great store by the *Malleus Malleficarum*, that tissue of lies and propaganda dreamt up by two Dominican Inquisitors to justify their unwholesome imaginings.

Rudd's 'Nine Hyerarchies of Angels with their Invocations to Visible Appearance' reminds one of the atmosphere of the John Dee and Edward Kelley workings. Dee and Kelley also were almost obsessively concerned with whether they had invoked a 'good' or 'evil' spirit, and went to great lengths to develop methods of working which could protect them against stray 'evil' spirits. Indeed, both Dee and Kelley remained uncertain, even years after they had ceased to work together on their Enochian magic, as to whether the spirits they had then contacted were 'good' or 'evil.'

The question of dualism is of great import in esotericism.

Western occultism has been much influenced by the Kabbalistic stream which, being the esoteric tradition of the Jewish peoples, could not help but have the polarized naive dualism of the Jewish patriarchal religion impressed into its symbolism and method of working. The formative idea of the Fall of Man being linked with a 'Fall' of rebel Angels, which then became 'Demons' bearing special relationship to Man, lay at the heart of this spiritual dualism. Norman Cohn, in his excellent book *Europe's Inner Demons* (1975), which I recommend to be read in conjunction with this Treatise, shows how this view was consolidated in history from the twelfth century and led to the establishment of a stereotyped picture of the Magician figure, conjuring Demons, making pacts with the Devil, etc., and later also regrettably brought about great suffering through the projection of such dualistic archetypes onto women, in the witchcraft persecutions.

With the greater understanding of the psyche that has arisen since the identification of the realm of the unconscious within our being, and the recognition by Jung and others that these different facets of the psyche must be integrated in order to avoid pathological conditions arising through repressing in a dualistic way a side of our being, esotericists and occultists in the twentieth century have been able to see more clearly the dangers of dualism and seek for a balanced esotericism.

It has, therefore, become obvious that occultists of an earlier time, especially during the transition of the middle ages into the Renaissance, were strongly influenced by the prevailing current of dualism that was given fresh energy through the impulse of naive Protestantism.

Before this period magicians could work naturally to invoke spirits without any great inner qualms. They saw that such spirits were, after all, part of God's creation and worthy of the occultist's attention. The earliest *grimoires*, the books of conjuration, describe elevated spiritual rituals that would not be out of place in any religious tradition, requiring fasting, abstention and a period of celibacy, prayers to God, purification and remission of sins, and petitions and addresses to the supreme God, in whose name they undertook their occult work. One suspects that few priests or bishops of the time took their church rituals quite so seriously as their magician contemporaries.

With the inpouring of the dualistic philosophical view into the collective consciousness, which one sees beginning in the twelfth century or thereabouts, these magical exercises or rituals are seen in a different light, both by outsiders to the experience and by the practitioners of the art itself. From that time on, ritual magic becomes plagued by dualism, and the magician's healthy relationship to the realm of spirits, his personal exploration through ritual of the spiritual world, becomes diseased by a concern about 'evil.'

This 'evil,' of course, we can see as being nothing else but an encounter of the magician with his unconscious mind, though it was to be many hundreds of years before this realm was recognized by our consciousness in such a way that the possibilities of an integrated relationship transcending dualism could come about.

Magical philosophy and ritual thus suffered an intrusion of the naive dualistic preoccupations of churchmen and scholars, struggling with their polarized patriarchal Christian religion whose internal contradictions were beginning to impinge upon their consciousness during the transition of the medieval period into the Renaissance.

The results of this struggle within the collective psyche of man can be seen mirrored in this *Treatise on Angel Magic*. Here, we have a compendium of material on 'Angels,' the spiritual beings of God (under a dualistic theology). But in order to fully describe these Angels and the means of working with them, Dr. Rudd has to outline a list of other spirits which under the same dualistic theology he must identify as 'Demons.' Thus he lists 'good' and 'evil' spirits, their characters and operation, and later has to expand at length on ways of avoiding working with 'evil' spirits.

It is interesting that he occasionally uses the word 'daemon' in place of 'demon,' where he experiences internal contradictions as to whether the being is 'good' or 'evil'. Thus Socrates' 'daemon'—his spiritual genius. In this earlier sense a 'daemon' meant a 'spirit' and was not colored with associations of good and evil.

The Treatise on Angel Magic gives us, in a sense, a thin slice of the collective psyche of Western humanity seen through the being of a magician who, sensitive to the reality of the existence of the realms of spiritual beings, nevertheless has to struggle with the prevailing naive dualism inherent in the Western religious tradition, which had been imported into his psyche. Rudd's struggle to unite these poles of dualism in his magical philosophy is quite transparent and should be of continuing interest in our time, when the process of integration, though collectively embarked upon, is in no sense completed. We can often witness our contemporaries descending into the same primitive dualisms that lived in and motivated peoples of earlier times, projecting such dualistic archetypes upon individuals, nations or events. This dualism which still lives in the atmosphere around us and within us, is perhaps the greatest problem that Western humanity has to face. We can only hope that an integration of these polarities in the Jungian sense can lead to a personal and societal 'individuation' that can heal this disease of the psyche.

The section on the Enochian tables is of great interest. The only primary published source of this is Casaubon's *A True and Faithful Relation of what passed for many years between Dr. John Dee and some Spirits* (1659), which is an edited version of some of Dee's Spiritual Diaries. It is certainly not a 'true and faithful relation,' but rather betrays Casaubon's hand in editing the material to show Dee in an unfavorable light. Casaubon was essentially a propagandist against Hermeticism and his motives in publishing his version of the Spiritual Diaries were to discredit Dee and tarnish his reputation. He even went so far as to describe it in his Preface as a 'work of darkness.' Included as a frontispiece illustration to his book is the famous diagram (shown on page 19) of the setting of the Holy Table with the enigmatic Enochian Squares around the sevenfold star. This was to be used in conjunction with the Seal of Aemeth, which I have included as a frontispiece illustration to this volume (the original wax version is still preserved in the British Museum), which tied together this sevenfold symbolism. However, the meaning of the letters and symbols on these squares has never been fully explained by any present day occultist, but I believe that the tradition which Rudd here records can be of value in helping scholars and esotericists to further unravel the intricacies of the system. It is especially important that, in the description of the Seven Tables, mention is made of two Angels from the *Steganographia* of Johannes Trithemius, thus for the first time providing documentary evidence that Dee's Enochian system bore some direct relationship to Trithemius' Angel Magic.

I have published this work because it seems to me to be an important compendium on Angel Magic, fairly summarizing the Western esoteric tradition at the end of the seventeenth century. Further, it includes the unique material on the Enochian Tables that is in itself of great value. Finally, I feel this work to be important to scholars and historians as its supposed author Dr. Rudd reveals the atmosphere of entrenched dualism within which he worked, which colored and charged his own perceptions, and no doubt those of his contemporaries. The Rudd Treatise was never meant to be published. It was, rather, a private 'commonplace book' or perhaps a reference book for a group or order of occultists working closely with Dr. Rudd. The Harley manuscript, as we realize, is merely a copy made in the early 1700's by Peter Smart, who was likely to have been one of Rudd's circle. The existence of this manuscript indicates the continuity of an occult system of Angel Magic, stretching from the workings of John Dee and Edward Kelley in the late sixteenth century into the early eighteenth century. I believe it to be an important link in the chain of the transmission of esoteric traditions.

For this edition of Harley 6482, I have transcribed the text in its entirety from the 283 folios of the original, and have not edited out any sections or otherwise interfered with the substance of the manuscript. In places I have modernized the spelling, but the style of the original is sufficiently close to modern usage not to require any editing. While working upon the manuscript I had the impression that certain sections were originally written in Latin and had been translated into English rather clumsily. It is also my view that this Treatise was intended as a compilation of the tradition of Angel Magic of the sixteenth and seventeenth centuries, for the use of a group of practicing occultists centered around Dr. Rudd. Hopefully, further historical research might help to identify this group and their means of working. The series of Rudd manuscripts in the

Harley Collection provides, I believe, a fascinating glimpse into the concerns and activities of the occultism of the late seventeenth century.

—ADAM MCLEAN

Bibliography

Agrippa, Henry Cornelius. *De Occulta Philosophia*, translated by J.F. and published as *Three Books of Occult Philosophy*, London 1651.

Barrett, Francis.*The Magus*, 1801.

Casaubon, Meric. *A True and Faithful Relation of what passed for many years between Dr John Dee... and some Spirits*, 1659.

Cavendish.*The Powers of Evil in Western Religion, Magic and Folk Belief*, 1975.

Cohn, Norman. *Europe's Inner Demons*, 1975.

Crowley, Aleister. "A Brief Abstract of the Symbolic Representation of the Universe," *The Equinox*, 1911.

French, Peter. *John Dee: The World of an Elizabethan Magus*, 1972.

The Magical Calendar, Edited by Adam McLean, Magnum Opus Hermetic Sourceworks, Number 1, 1979; New and revised edition, 1990.

Trithemius, Johannes. *The Steganographia of Johannes Trithemius*, edited by Adam McLean, Magnum Opus Hermetic Sourceworks, Number 12, 1982.

Walker, D.P. *Spiritual and Demonic Magic*, 1958.

Yates, Frances. *The Rosicrucian Enlightenment*, 1975.

Yates, Frances. *The Occult Philosophy in the Elizabethan Age*, 1979.

THE HOLY TABLE
as laid out for the Angelic Invocations
of John Dee and Edward Kelley

Frontispiece from Casaubon's
"True and Faithful Relation..."

This frontispiece illustration to Harley 6482 was drawn by Peter Smart. It would appear to be a picture of a mirror glass, placed upon a three-legged stand with its back turned outwards towards the reader. This back is extremely ornate and embellished with various figures and Hebrew names. Thus we see the first seven letters of the Angelic Alphabet, Agiel to Graphiel, and the seventy-two Schemhamphoras in Hebrew letters arranged in a series of ribbons amongst the chase-work. At the top upon the handle of the mirror we note the 'Secret Sigil of Solomon' surrounded by a circle of smaller sigils and letters. Most likely, Peter Smart was indicating by this figure some of the keys to the Angel Magic outlined by Rudd in his treatise, part of which involves using a magic mirror for the Invocation of the Nine Hierarchies to visible appearance.—*Editor*

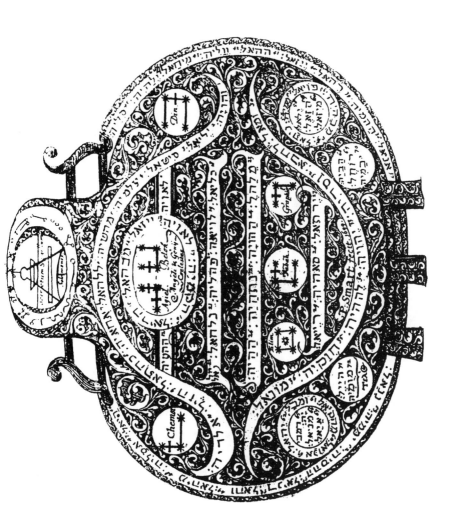

A TREATISE

ON

ANGEL MAGIC

being a complete transcription
of Ms Harley 6482 in the
British Library

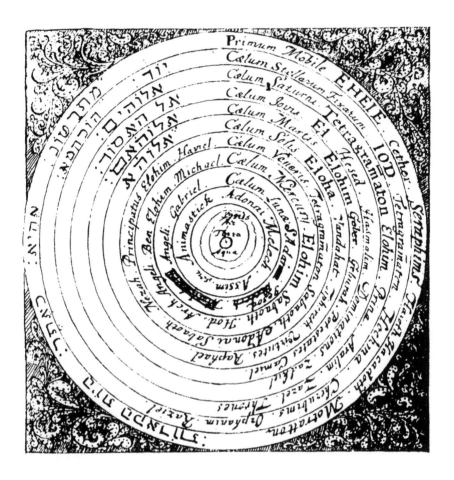

The Ten Names of God, with their Ideas, Orbs and Hierarchies Largely Explained

God himself though he be trinity in persons yet is but one only simple Essence, there are in him many Divine powers, which as many beams flow from him which the Philosophers of the Gentiles called Gods.

The first name of the Divine Essence is EHEIE and his Idea is called Cether, which signifies a Crown, the most simple Essence of the Divinity which the Eye seeth not and is attributed to God the Father and hath his influence by the Order of Seraphims, who the Hebrews call Hayoth Hecadoth, that is, Creatures of Holiness, and then by the Primum Mobile bestoweth the gift of being to all things filling the whole Universe, both through the Circumference and Centre, whose particular Intelligence is called Metratton, that is, the Prince of Faces, whose duty is to bring others to the face of the Prince, and by him the Lord spake to Moses.

The second name is JOD or Tetragrammaton. His Idea is Hochma, that is, Wisdom, and signifieth the Divinity full of Ideas, and the first begotten, and is attributed to the Son, and hath his influence by the Order of Cherubims, which the Hebrews call Ophanim, that is forms or wheels, and from thence into the starry heaven where he fabricateth so many figures as he has Ideas in himself, and distinguisheth the very Chaos of the Creatures by particular Intelligence called Raziel who was the ruler of Adam.

The third name is called TETRAGRAMMATON ELOHIM. His Idea is named Bina, viz., Providence and Understanding, and signifies Remission, quietness, the Jubilee, penitential Conversion, a great trumpet, Redemption of the world, and the life of the world to come. It is attributed to the Holy Spirit and hath influence by the Order of Thrones, which the Hebrews call Aralim, that is, great Angels, mighty and strong, and from thence by the sphere of Saturn administreth form to the unsettled matter, whose particular Intelligence is Zaphkiel or Zazel the Ruler of Noah, and another Intelligence named Iophiel, the Ruler of Sem. And these are three supreme and high Ideas, as it were seats of the Divine Persons, by whose command all things are made, but are executed by the other seven upon Earth, which are therefore called the divine Ideas framing.

The fourth name is EL whose Idea is Hesed, which is Clemency or goodness, and signifies Grace, Mercy, piety, magnificence, the Sceptre and right hand, and hath his influence by the Order of Dominions, which the Hebrews call Hasmalim, and so through the sphere of Jupiter, fashioning the Images of bodies, bestowing Clemency and pacifying Justice on all. His particular Intelligence is Zadkiel, the Ruler of Abraham.

The fifth name is ELOHIM GIBOR, that is the mighty God punishing the wicked, and his Idea is called Geburah, that is, power, gravity, fortitude, severity, Judgement, punishing by slaughter and war, and it is applied to the tribunal of God. The Girdle, the Sword, and the left hand of God, it is called Pachad, which is fear, and has his influence through the Order of Powers, which the Hebrews call Seraphim; and these through the sphere of Mars illuminate the Rosy Crucians to whom belongs fortitude and prudence. It draweth forth the Elements, and his particular Intelligence is Camiel the Ruler of Sampson.

The sixth name is ELOHA or a name of והבה joined with Vandabat, his Idea is Tiphareth, that is Apparel, beauty, glory, pleasure, and signifieth the tree of life, and hath his influence through the Order of Virtues, which the Hebrews call Malachim, that is, Angels, into the Sphere of the Sun, giving brightness and life unto it, and from thence producing metals and thereto make aurum potabile. His particular Intelligence is Raphael who was the Ruler of Isaac and Toby the younger, and the Angel Peliel Ruler of Jacob.

The seventh name is TETRAGRAMMATON SABAOTH or Adonai Sabaoth, that is the God of Hosts, and his Idea is Nezah, that is, triumph and victory. It signifies the eternity and Justice of a revenging God, he hath his influence through the Order of Principalities, whom the Hebrews call Elohim, that is, Lords, into the sphere of Venus. Gives Zeal and Love of righteousness, and produceth vegetables. His Intelligence is Haniel, and the Angel Cerviel the Ruler of David.

The eighth name is ELOHIM SABAOTH, which is interpreted the God of Hosts, not of war and justice but of piety and agreement; for his name signifieth both, and proceedeth his army. The Idea of this is Hod which is interpreted both praise, confession, honour and famousness, it hath influence through the Order of Archangels, which the Hebrews call Ben Elohim, that is the Sons of God, into the sphere of Mercury and gives eligancy and consonancy of speech and produceth living creatures. His Idea is Michael who was the Ruler of Salomon.

The ninth name is called SADAI, that is, Omnipotent, satisfying all, and Elhai, which is the living God. His Idea is Jesod, that is, foundation and rest, and hath his influence through the Order of Angels, whom the Hebrews call Cherubim, into the sphere of the Moon causing the increase and decrease of things and taketh care of the Ideas of the Earth, of the Rulers of the Twelve Divisions and of their Images or figures and of the Genii and keepers of men and distributeth them. His Genius is Gabriel who was the keeper of Joseph, Joshua and Daniel.

The tenth name is ADONAI MELECH, that is Lord and King, his Idea is Malcuth, that is Kingdom and Empire, and signifieth Church, Temple of God and a Gate, and hath his influence through the Order of Anamastick, viz., of blessed Souls, which by the Hebrews is called Assim, that is Nobles, Lords and Squires, they are inferior to the Hyerarchies and have their influence in the sixteen figures of Geomancy, the twelve Ideas, the four Elements and their twelve Regions or places divided, the twelve Winds which come forth from the twelve Houses of the Earth and on the Sons of Men. And thus they give knowledge, and the wonderful understanding of things, industry and predictions, and the President among them is Methratton, which is called the first Creature or the Soul of the World, and Sorath or ⊙ distributeth his virtues. And after this manner do the Earthly powers receive their Commissions which are figuratively incorporated into seven and they again in their natures given it to twelve, which also in twelve places signify all things past, present and to come in all the world.

In the Intelligible World according to Dionysius, these are the names of the ten Orders of the Blessed:

1 Seraphims
2 Cherubims
3 Thrones
4 Dominations
5 Powers
6 Virtues
7 Principalities
8 Archangels
9 Angels
10 Blessed Souls

According to the Hebrew Rabbins the ten Orders bear these names:

1 Haioth Hakadoth
2 Ophani
3 Aralim
4 Hasmalim
5 Seraphim
6 Malachim
7 Elohim
8 Ben Elohim
9 Cherubim
10 Issim

And these Orders possess the ten Spheres of the World, which are these:

1 The Primum Mobile or first mover
2 The Sphere of the Zodiac
3 The Sphere of Saturn
4 The Sphere of Jupiter
5 The Sphere of Mars
6 The Sphere of the Sun
7 The Sphere of Venus
8 The Sphere of Mercury
9 The Sphere of the Moon
10 The Sphere of the Elements

Anima Mundi – The Soul of the World

All the Platonics and Pythagoreans, Orpheus, Trismegistus, Aristotle, Theophrastus, Avicenna, Algazales and all Peripatetics acknowledge and confirm that the world is not only inhabited by spirit and soul but also by the participation of the Divine Mind, and all origin, virtue and vigour of inferior things depends upon this Anima Mundi.

The Magi call the Anima Mundi or the whole Universe, the realm of Jove; indeed they name it the Apollonian mind of the world; and moreover the Minerva Nature of the world, in fire Vulcan, in water Neptune, and they have called it by many names.

Also the Pythagoreans set twelve particular Gods of the Zodiac, or such souls situated in the hearts of the stars, and accordingly we can write all the rulers of the stars as:

Pallas, particularly in the heart of Aries,
Venus, particularly in the heart of Taurus,
Phoebus, particularly of Gemini,
Mercury of Cancer,
Jupiter of Leo,
Ceres of Virgo,
Vulcan of Libra,
Mars of Scorpio,
Diana of Sagittarius,
Vesta of Capricorn,
Juno particularly of Aquarius,
Neptune particularly in the soul of Pisces.

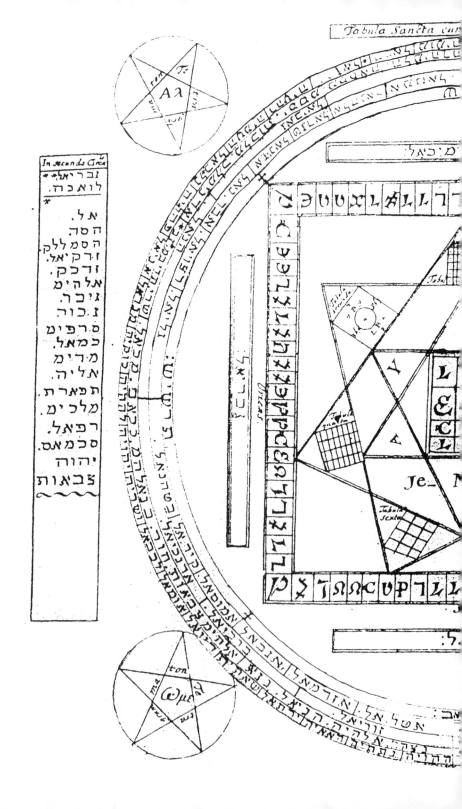

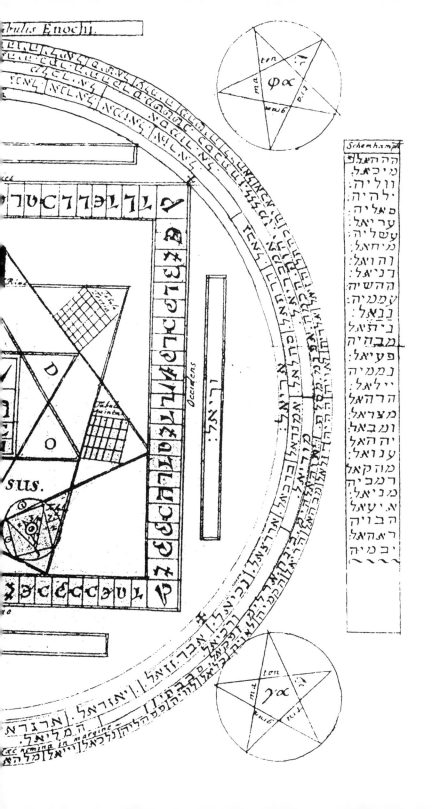

The Characters of the Sixteen Figures of Geomancy Expressed in the Great and Lesser Squares of Tabula Sancta

The figures Septentrional V ʒ ꓶ etc, in number 23, relate to the fourth and fifth Tables.

The figures Oriental V ꓔ Ɣ etc, relate to the second and third Tables.

The figures Meridional V Ɣ b etc, relate to the first Table.

The figures Occidental V ʒ Ɛ etc, relate to the sixth and seventh Tables.

These characters represent the seven Rulers of the Earth with their Twelve Ideas which are attributed to the twelve Regions of the Earth contained in the Sixteen figures of Geomancy.

V signifies Malchidael ⁙ Puer — a figure of Barzabel or Mars in Aries.

ʒ signifies Hasmodel ⁘ Amissio — a figure of Kedemel or Venus in Taurus.

ꓶ signifies Ambriel or ⁑ Albus — a figure of Taphthartarath or Mercury in Gemini.

Ω signifies Muriel or ⦂⦂ Populus — a figure of Hasmodai or the Moon in Cancer, increasing.

ꓔ signifies Muriel or ⦂ Via — a figure of Hasmodai or the Moon in Cancer, decreasing.

b signifies Verchiel or ⦂⁝ Fortuna Major — a figure of Sorath or the Sun in Capricorn, in Northern Declination.

Ϸ signifies Advachiel or ⁝⦂ Fortuna Minor — a figure of Sorath or the Sun in Leo in Southern Declination.

ꓶ signifies Hamaliel or ⁚⁚ Conjuntio — a figure of Taphthartarath, or Mercury in Virgo.

∠ signifies Zuriel or ⦙⦙ Puella — a figure of Kedemel or Venus in Libra.

Ɣ signifies Barchiel or ⦂⦂ Rubeus — a figure of Barzabel or Mars in Scorpio.

♃ signifies Advachiel or ⁂ Acquisitio — a figure of Hismael or Jupiter in Sagittarius.

ה signifies Hanael or ⁚⁚ Carcer — a figure of Zazel or Saturn in Capricorn. (ה)

ε signifies Cambriel or ⁚⁚ Tristitia — a figure of Hismael or Saturn in Aquarius.

ɞ signifies Amnixiel or ⁚⁚ Laetitia — a figure of Hismael or Jupiter in Pisces.

⟋ signifies Hismael and Kedemel in all their Ideas being a figure of ⁎⁎⁎ or Caput Draconis.

⤳ signifies Zazel and Barzabel in all their Ideas being a figure of ⁝ or Cauda Draconis.

Observe that every part of the square, or a quarter of Heaven is governed by 18 spirits mentioned in the Schemhamphoras hereafter following, which spirits are partly good and partly evil.

ORATIO

O Angeli gloriosi in hac Quadra Scripti estote coadjutores et auxiliatores meos in omnibus Questionibus et interrogationibus Resolvendis, in omnibus negotiis caeterisque causis per eum qui venturus est judicare vivos, et mortuos, et mundum per ignem.

The First Table of Enoch hath relation to the South part of the Square governed by Michael.

The Second and Third Tables of Enoch have relation to the East part of the Square governed by Gabriel and Uriel.

The Fourth and Fifth Tables of Enoch have relation to the East and West part of the Square governed by Gabriel and Uriel.

The Sixth and Seventh Tables of Enoch have relation to the North part of the Square governed by Raphael.

These Tables as well as the second and seventh are charged with Spirits or Genii both good and bad of several Orders and Hierarchies, which the wise King Solomon made use of.

THE FIRST TABLE OF ENOCH
divided into 40 Mansions or Squares.
TABULA LUNAE.

2 buer ✝ botis	Gaap botis buer	Glasia Labolas	22 leg Botis	Bathin 24 leg botis buer bael	botis buer Lobquise Buer	Balam 101 leg	Belial
botis bael buer balam 8	Gaap botis 8	bael buer	gaap gaap botis	buer	bael	62 leg bael Belial Balam	Belial ✝ Bael
Chamiel q* 5 C leg Bael q* / bael Ose / Ose otiel		Belial 2.9	Buer 9 times invocated	Valac Belial 5	Buer 5 times	bael 3 times	Botis 3 times 83 leg
Buer 6	Botis	Buer murmur 166 leg	buer	bael	Caim murmur	Belial	buer Amaimon 155 bael
buer	Belial	bune	buer Tetra-gramaton	4 times Belial Bael q*	Belial Bael Balam buer botis	buer botis 72 leg Furcas	bael

*q stands for quingent

Intelligentia Intelligentiarum Lunae—
Malcha Betharissimi hod bervah.
Demonium Lunae— Schedbarscemoth Scharththam.

THE SECOND TABLE OF ENOCH
TABULA MERCURII

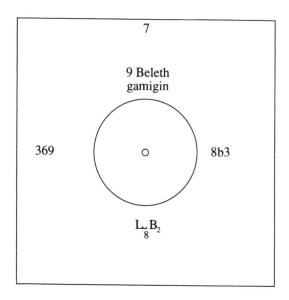

Intelligentia Mercurii: שיריאל
Daemonium Mercurii — תחהתרשרת Taphthatarath

(7) denoted Cassiel in the 7th Orb or Heaven of Saturn in the Order of the Thrones.

(8) shows Methratton in the 9th Heaven. Bilieth attends there and Gamigin.

(3) shows Anael and Bune 9 times to be invoked.

(8) shows Raziel in the starry firmament in the Order of Cherubims 3 times to be invoked.

Underneath is placed $L.B_2$ that is to say, Larmol that is one of the 12 Dukes that waits on Caspiel, a great Emperor ruling in the South, and with him appears Budarym, twice to be invoked. [See Chapter XVIII of *The Steganographia of Johannes Trithemius*— Editor.]

As Cassiel governs the head of the square, so Raziel governs the bottom.

THE THIRD TABLE OF ENOCH
divided into 36 squares.
TABULA VENERIS

5 Paimon Bathin 4 Purson	Astaroth Ebra	Bune Diriel	Barbatos Loraje	Botis Pamersiel	Berith Glasia Labolas
Barbatos Loraie	Barbatos Otiel	Buer 6	Bathin Loraie	Bathin Sitri	Bathin Valefar
Bileth Bathin	Bune Caim 3	Balam Murmur	Belial Vepar	Bifrons Forcator	Belial Bifrons Forcator
3 Berith Astaroth2	Buer Caim 3	Bonoha Bune 3 8 Buer	Belial 8	Belial 7	Belial 5
Belial 6	Belial 4	Belial 1	Belial 9	Buer bune otiel	Belial 3
Belial Balam	Belial Bathin 262 leg	Belial 7 Astaroth	686 leg Marcho-sias	Belial Balam	Buer bune 867 leg

THE FOURTH TABLE OF ENOCH
contains 32 mansions.
TABULA SOLIS

Gaap Damael 2 Gabriel	Bilet Loraiel 30 leg	buer | Bael 8 | 2	Belial Ose	Balam Osael	Ose Laquel buer 9 9.29	Balay 82 leg	galdel baliol Bachanael
Ose porna Baciel 98 leg	✠ 9 ∩ Balidet	buer 2 8 Gaap	bael 2 Rael	Buer 3 2 Rahumel	bilel 11 Raphael	Belial Balam 12 leg Turiel	buer bael 9 Friagne
Baliel Balay buer gaap	Michael 2	Masgabiel	Malayel	Dam|ael 2 Bac- iel 7	Mathiel	Atel 6 | 3	Bebel Bael Buer 2
Mitraton buel 9:9 Laquel	buer bael ✠ 4.6	bilet 9 ✠	buer bael	6 | Bael 2 | 4	Hyniel Balidet 38 leg	Nelapa Bilet 9	bilet buer 4 bael

In the 10th Mansion of the Fourth Table you find ∩ which signifies Caspiel who is the highest and greatest Emperor ruling in the South.

THE FIFTH TABLE OF ENOCH
contains 24 Mansions or squares.
TABULA MARTIS

buer $\frac{2}{2}$ baal	buer buer Ose	537 leg buer buer buer	buel Belial gemori valac	Turiel 13 leg buer buer buer	buer 9 times
Deamiel 4 Baraborat	Ose 4 Belial bathin	Bileth 14 ☾	Botis buer bileth Paimon 3	barbatos Gamigin Ophiel	buer botis Cimeriel Vual
8 Camuel Bealpharos	Och Ose 7 buer bael	♂ ♂	99	99 Balam	buer Loraie
Gemori Ose 36 leg Belial	9.3 buer bael	99 5 buer botis	♆ 6	7.2 buer Barbatos	Bileth Bathin .⋀. 8 3

In the 15th Mansion of the Fifth Table you find ♂ which signifies the Spirit Bealphares.

In the 22nd Mansion of the Fifth Table you find ♆ which is the seal of Pamersiel.

In the 24th Mansion of the Fifth Table you find ⋀ which is the seal of Asmodai.

THE SIXTH TABLE OF ENOCH
consists of twelve squares or Mansions.
TABULA JOVIS

┼┼ Gabriel Bilet 28 leg	Michael 30 9 Osael Babel Gabrael	999 Rael Osael Babel Gabrael
Berith ઘ The five Kings of the North: Sitrael Malantha Thamaor Sitrami Gusoin	┼┼ Baliel ─O Arcan	Lobquin hyniel Balay Galdel Osael
Asmodai ☾ 5 Buer Padiel ℛ	Mathiel Dabriel darquiel buer 2 Amaimon	Laquel 30 leg buer paimon paidiel
Valac 9 times hyniel bilet 22 leg	9 ♌ 9 baer amon 9 gusoin ose	25 leg Baraborat Lama damael

Intelligentia Jovis : יוסהיאל Jophiel.
Daemonium Jovis : היסמאל Hismael.

In this Table in the third square or Mansion I find (999 R) shows that 1200 ministering spirits attending Rael are sometimes invocated and ready to obey, for where you find 9 it signifies quadringeni the like of two.

THE SEVENTH TABLE OF ENOCH

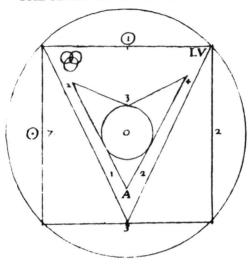

Intelligentia Saturni : אגיאל Agiel.
Daemonium Saturni : זאזל Zazel.

Within the Circle ① is signified the first Orb or Heaven of Luna in the Order of Angels wherein resides and governs that glorious ministering Angel Gabriel. On the left side of the square is ☉ where Michael and Uriel reside in the 4th Orb or Heaven of Sol in the Order of Virtues, and over against it is 2, which shows the second Orb or Heaven of Mercury in the Order of Archangels.

Underneath is 3, showing the third Orb or Heaven where resides Anael of the Order of Principalities.

Within the square is ♃ showing the great mystery of the Trinity. In an infinite Circle or Orb within the square is a Triangle pointing downwards, and signifies the Microcosm or little world, man, made up of Salt, Sulphur and Mercury, and note that within the ▽ is this figure ☿ which demonstrates that all animals are composed of Salt, Sulphur and Mercury. The figure about the Microcosm imports that Man is a Trinity composed of the four Elements, that he hath, first a Vegetative, second a Sensitive, third a Rational, Soul. 'A' underneath the ▽ signifies Animus Corpus vivens sentiens rationale.

'7' within the square shows Cassiel or Zaphkiel in the seventh Orb or Heaven of Saturn in the Order of the Thrones. On one side of the ▽ is ⊛ which signifies the Seal of Sibillia, the gentle Virgin of the Fairies and at the opposite end is placed 'LV', i.e. Leraiv Valefar.

Note that some of these spirits are to be Invocated as often as they are repeated by numerical figures not exceeding 9 times.

All these Angels are in Hebrew included in a Circle round the Table.

The names of the Angels presiding over the Planets:

Saturn	Zaphkiel
Jupiter	Zadkiel
Mars	Camiel
Sun	Raphael
Venus	Haniel
Mercury	Michael
Moon	Gabriel

These are the seven which always stand before the face of God, which are believed to be stationed in the entire heavenly realm and in the Earthly which is below the orbit of the Moon.

Round the Circles of Enoch's Tables

The Angel Presidents of the twelve signs are assuredly in command of the twelve signs:

Aries	Malchidael
Taurus	Asmodel
Gemini	Ambriel
Cancer	Muriel
Leo	Verchiel
Virgo	Hamaliel
Libra	Zuriel
Scorpio	Barbiel
Sagittarius	Advachiel
Capricorn	Hanael
Aquarius	Gambiel
Pisces	Barchiel

The Twenty Eight Angels which rule in the Twenty Eight
Mansions of the Moon which are named in order

1 Geniel	10 Ardesiel	20 Kiriel
2 Enediel	11 Nociel	21 Bethnael
3 Amnixiel	12 Abduxuel	22 Geliel
4 Azariel	13 Jazeriel	23 Requiel
5 Cabiel	14 Ergodiel	24 Abrinael
6 Dirachiel	15 Ataliel	25 Aziel
7 Scheliel	16 Azeruel	26 Tagriel
8 Amnediel	17 Adriel	27 Alhoniel
9 Barbiel	18 Egibiel	28 Amnixiel
	19 Amutiel	

The Four Angels of the Winds set over the parts of the World
Michael is governor over the East Wind
Raphael over the West Wind
Gabriel over the North Wind
Nariel, who is called by others Uriel, is over the South Wind.

The Angels of the Elements

Air	Cherub
Water	Tharsis
Earth	Ariel
Fire	Seraph (or just the same as Philonem Nathaniel)

The Four Most Powerful Kings
in command over the rest of the evil spirits are named

Uricus	King of the East
Amaymon	King of the South
Paymon	King of the West
Egyn	King of the North

These the Hebrew doctors by chance called correctly,

Samael   Azazel   Azael   Mahazael

The Schemhamphoras

The Schemhamphoras are seventy two Angels that bear the Name of God. These Names are included in certain sentences of Scripture and expressed at the end of every verse, which verses are used sometimes as occasion requires when invocation is made for visible appearance.

1   Tu Domine susceptor meus es gloria mea et exaltans Caput meum: וחויאה **Vehujah** — Thou, O Lord, art my guardian, and exaltest my head.

2   Et tu Domine ne elongaveris auxilium tuum a me, ad defensionem meam conspice: יליאל **Ieliel** — Do not remove thy help from me, O Lord, and look to my defense.

3   Dicam Domino susceptor meus es tu, et refugium meum Deus meus sperabo in sum: סיראל **Sirael** — I shall say to the Lord, Thou art my guardian, my God is my refuge, and I shall hope in him.

4   Convertere Domino, et eripe animam meam, salvum me fac propter misericordiam tuam: אלמיאל **Elemijel** — Turn, O Lord, and deliver my soul, and save me for Thy mercy's sake.

5   Psalite Domino qui habitat in Sion annunciate inter gentes studia eius: ללהאל **Lelahel** — Let him who lives in Zion sing unto the Lord, and proclaim his goodwill among the peoples.

6   Miserator et misericors Dominus, longanimus et multum misericors: אכאיאה **Achajah** — The Lord is merciful and compassionate, long-suffering and of great goodness.

7   Ex qui sive Dominum et exaudivit me, et ex omnibus tribulationibus eripuit me : מהשייה **Mahasiah** — I called upon the Lord and he heard me and delivered me from all my tribulations.

8   Venite, adoremus, et procidamus ante Dominum qui ferit

nos: כהשאל **Cahatel** — O come let us adore and fall down before God
who bore us.

9   Reminiscere miserationum tuarum Domine et miserationum tuarum quae a saeculo sunt: חֲזִיאֵל **Haziel** — Remember Thy
mercies, O Lord, and Thy mercies which have been for ever.

10   Fiat misericordia tua super nos, quemadmodu speravimus
in te: אלדיה **Aladiah** — Perform Thy mercies upon us, for we have
hoped in Thee.

11   Vivit Dominus et benedictus Deus meus et exaltatur Deus
salutis meae: לאויאה **Laviah** — The Lord liveth, blessed is my God,
and let the God of my salvation be exalted.

12   Ut quid Domine recessisti longe desperis in opportunitati-
bus in tribulatione: הֲהִיה **Hahajah** — Why hast Thou departed, O
Lord, so long from us perishing in the times of tribulation.

13   Jubilate Domino omnis Terra, Cantate, et exultate, et
Psallite: יְלָאֵל **Jezalel** — Rejoice in the Lord, all ye lands, sing, exult,
and play upon a stringed instrument.

14   Et factus est Dominus refugium, et Deus meus in adjutorium spei meae: מבהאל **Mebahel** — The Lord is a refuge, and my God
the help of my hope.

15   Et factus est mihi Dominus in refugium et Deus meus in
adjutorium spei meae: הֲרִיאֵל **Hariel** — The Lord is a refuge for me
and my God the help of my hope.

16   Domine Deus salutis meae in die clamavi et nocte coram
te: הקמיה **Hakamiah** — O Lord, God of my salvation, by day have I
called to thee, and sought Thy presence by night.

17   Domine Dominus noster quam admirabile est nomen
tuum in universa terra: לאויה **Leviah** — O Lord our Lord, How
wonderful is Thy name in all the world.

18   Iudica me Domine secundum misericordiam et iustitiam

tuam Domine Deus meus et non supergaudeant mihi: בְּלִיאֵל **Caliel** — Judge me, O Lord, according to Thy loving kindness, and let not them be joyful over me, O Lord.

19 Expectans expectavi Dominum et intendit mihi: לָוִויָה **Luviah** — I waited in hope for the Lord, and He turned to me.

20 Et nomen Domini invocabo O Domine libera animam meam: פַּהֲלִיָה **Pahaliah** — I shall call upon the name of the Lord, O Lord free my soul.

21 Ego autem in te speravi Domine dixi Deus meus es tu: וְלְכָאֵל **Nelakhel** — In Thee also have I hoped, O Lord, and said, Thou art my God.

22 Dominus custodit te, Dominus protectio tua super manum dextram tuam: יְיָאֵל **Jajajel** — The Lord keep thee, the Lord be thy protection on thy right hand.

23 Dominus custodit introitum tuum et exitum tuum ex nunc et usque in saeculum: מֶלְהָאֵל **Melahel** — The Lord keep thine incoming and thine outgoing from this time forth for evermore.

24 Beneplacitum est Domino super timentes eum, et in iis qui sperant super misericordiam eius: חֲהֵיָה **Hahajah** — The Lord is well pleased with those that fear Him and hope upon his mercy.

25 Confitebor tibi Domine in tote corde meo narrabo omnia mirabilia tua: נְחְהָיָה **Nithhajah** — I shall acknowledge Thee, O Lord, with all my heart and shall tell forth all Thy wonders.

26 Clamavi in toto corde meo, exaudi me Domine, iustificationes meas requiram: הָאִיָה **Haajah** — I have called unto Thee with all my heart, hear me, O Lord, and I shall seek my justification.

27 Eripe me Domine ab homine malo a viro iniquo eripe me: ירְחָאֵל **Jerathel** — Save me, O Lord, from the evil man and deliver me from the wicked doer.

28 Deus ne elongeris a me Deus meus in auxilium meum

respice: שאחיה **Sehijah** — Let not God depart from me, look to my help, O God.

29   Ecce Deus adiuvat me et Dominus susceptor est animae meae: רייאל **Rejajel** — Behold, God is my helper, and the Lord is the guardian of my soul.

30   Quoniam tu es potentia mea Domine. Domine spes mea a iuventute mea: אומאל **Omael** — For Thou are my strength, O Lord. O Lord, Thou art my hope from my youth.

31   Introibo in potentia Domini, Deus meus memorabor iustitiae tuae solius: לכבאל **Lecabel** — I shall enter into the power of the Lord, my God, I shall be mindful of Thy justice only.

32   Quia rectum est verbum Domini et omnia opera eius in fide: ושריה **Vasariah** — For the word of the Lord is upright, and all his works faithful.

33   Dominus scit cogitationes hominum quoniam vana sunt: יהויה **Jehuvajah** — The Lord knows the thoughts of men, for they are in vain.

34   Speret Israel in Domino ex hoc nunc et usque in saeculum: להחיה **Lehahiah** — Let Israel hope in the Lord from this time forth and for evermore.

35   Dilexi quoniam exaudi Dominus vocem orationis meae: בוקיה **Chavakiah** — I am joyful, for the Lord hears the voice of my prayer.

36   Domini dilexi decorum domus tuae et locem habitationis gloriae tuae: מנדאל **Manadel** — I have delighted in the beauty of Thy House, O Lord, and in the place of the habitation of Thy glory.

37   Domine Deus virtutum converte nos et ostende faciem tuam et salvi erimus: אניאל **Aniel** — O Lord God, turn Thy power towards us, and show us Thy face and we shall be saved.

38   Quoniam tu es Domine spes mea altissimum profuisti

refugium tuum: הַעֲמִיָה **Haamiah** — For Thou art my hope, O Lord, and Thou hast been my deepest refuge.

39 Audivit Dominus et misertus est mihi Dominus factus est adiutor meus: רְחָאֵל **Rehael** — The Lord has heard me and pitied me and the Lord is my helper.

40 Ut quid Domine repellis animam meam, avertis faciem tuam a me: יְיָאֵל **Jejazel** — Why drivest Thou away my soul, O Lord, and turnest Thy face from me?

41 Domine libera animam meam a labiis iniquis et a lingua dolosa: הַחַאֵל **Hahahel** — O Lord, deliver my soul from wicked lips and a deceitful tongue.

42 Domine custodit te ab omni malo et custodiet animam tuam: מִיכָאֵל **Michael** — The Lord protects thee from all evil and will protect they soul.

43 Et Ego ad te Domine clamavit, et mane oratio meae praeveniet te: וְלִיָה **Vevaliah** — I have cried unto Thee, O Lord, and let my prayer come unto Thee.

44 Voluntaria eris mei beneplacita fac Domine et Judicia tua doce: יְלְבִיָה **Jelabiah** — Make my wishes pleasing unto Thee, O Lord, and teach me Thy judgments.

45 Si dicebam motus est pes meus misericordia tua Domine adiuvabit me: סָאלִיָה **Sealiah** — If I say that my foot is moved, Thou wilt help me of Thy mercy.

46 Suavis Dominus universis et miserationes super omnia opera eius: עֲרִיאֵל **Ariel** — The Lord is pleasant to all the world and his mercies are over all his works.

47 Quam magnificata sunt opera tua Domine, nimis profundae factae sunt cogitationes tuae: עֲשָׁלִיָה **Asaliah** — How wonderful are Thy works, O Lord, and how deep Thy thoughts.

48 Notum fecit Dominus salutare tuum in conspectu gen-

tium, revelabit justitiam suam: מיחאל **Michael** — The Lord hath made thy salvation known in the sight of the peoples and will reveal his justice.

49 Magnus Domine et laudabilis et magnitudinis eius non est finis: וְהוּאֵל **Vehael** — Great is the Lord and worthy to be praised, and there is no end to his greatness.

50 Miserator et misericors Dominus, patiens et multum misericors: דְּנִיאֵל **Daniel** — The Lord is pitiful and merciful, long-suffering and of great goodness.

51 Sit gloria Dominus in saeculu laetabitur Dominus in operibus suis: הַחֲשִׁיָה **Hahasiah** — Let the Lord be in glory for ever and the Lord will rejoice in His works.

52 Confitebor Domino sacundum justitiam eius et Psallam nomini Domini altissimi: עֲמָמִיָה **Iamamiah** — I shall make known the Lord, according to his justice, and sing hymns to the name of the Lord, the greatest.

53 Cognovi Domine quia aequitas judicia tua et in veritate tua humiliasti me: נְאָאֵל **Nanael** — I have known Thee, O Lord, for Thy judgments are just, and in Thy truth have I abased myself.

54 Dominus in Caelo paravit sedem suam et Regnum suum omnibus dominabitur: נִיתְאֵל **Nithael** — The Lord hath prepared His seat in heaven and His rule shall be over all.

55 Tu autem Domine in aeternum permanes et memoriale tuum in generationem et generationem: מֶבְהִיָה **Mebahiah** — Thou remainest for ever, O Lord, and Thy memorial is from generation to generation.

56 Allevat Dominus omnes qui corrunt, et erigit onmes elisos: פּוּלִיל **Polial** — The Lord raiseth up all who fall and setteth up the broken.

57 Qui timent Dominum speraverunt in Domino, adiutor eorum et protector eorem est: וְמָמִיָה **Nemamiah** — They who fear the

Lord have hoped in the Lord, He is their helper and their protector.

58 Et anima mea turbata est valde sed tu Domine usque quo: יֵילָאֵל Jejalel — My soul is greatly troubled, but Thou, O Lord art here also.

59 Ab ortu Solis usque ad occasum laudabile nomen Domini: הרחאל Harahel — From the rising of the Sun to the going down of the same, the word of the Lord is worthy to be praised.

60 Iustus Dominus in omnibus viis suis et sanctus in omnibus operibus eius: מצראל Mizrael — The Lord is just in all his ways and blessed in all his works.

61 Sit nomen Domini benedictum ex hoc nunc et usque in saeculum: ומבאל Umbael — Let the name of the Lord be blessed from this time forth for evermore.

62 Vide quoniam mandata tua Domine dilexi secundum misericordiam vivificam: יהחאל Iahael — See, O Lord, how I have delighted in Thy commandements according to Thy life-giving mercy.

63 Servite Domino in Laetitia, introite in conspectu eius in exultatione: עֲנוֹאֵל Anaviel — Serve ye the Lord with gladness and enter into his sight with exultation.

64 Ecce oculi Domini super metuentes eum et in eis qui sperant super misericordiam eius: מהקאל Mehikiel — Behold the eyes of the Lord are upon those that fear Him and hope in His loving kindness.

65 Convertere Domine usque quo et deprecabilis esto super servos eius: דמביה Damabiah — Turn, O Lord, even here also, and be pleased with Thy servants.

66 Ne derelinquas me Domine Deus meus ne discesseris a me: מֲנִיאֵל Meniel — Neither leave me, O Lord, nor depart from me.

67 Delectare in Domino et dabit tibi petitiones cordis tui:

אִיעָאֵל **Ejael** — Delight in the Lord and He will give thee the petitions of thy heart.

68 Confitemini Domino quoniam bonus, quoniam in aeternam misericordia eius: הַבְוִיה **Habujah** — Confess to the Lord, for He is God, and His mercy is for ever.

69 Dominus pars haereditatis meae et calicis meae tu es qui restitues haereditatem meam mihi: רֹאהאֵל **Roehel** — The Lord is my inheritance and my cup and it is Thou who restorest mine inheritance.

70 In principio creavit Deus Caelum et Terram: יִבָמִיה **Jabamiah** — In the beginning God created the heaven and the earth.

71 Confitebor Domino nimis in ore meo, et in medio multorum laudabo eum: הַיִיאֵל **Hajael** — I shall confess to the Lord with my mouth and praise Him in the midst of the multitude.

72 Convertere anima mea in requiem tuam quoniam Dominus benefaciet tibi: מוּמִיה **Mumijah** — Return to thy rest, my soul, for the Lord doeth thee good.

The Names of Some of the Good and Bad Spirits Solomon Made Use of

which are mentioned in Enoch's Seven Tables,
with a true account of their shapes, powers, government and
effects, with their several seigniories and degrees.

1 **AMAIMON**, King of the East.

2 **ATEL**, Angel of the fifth heaven.

3 **ASMODAI**, hath one Idea called Muriel incorporated into
two figures Geomantic, called Populus by day and Via by night. A
Lunar spirit.

4 **ASTAROTH**, a great and strong Duke coming forth in the
shape of a foul Angel, sitting upon an infernal Dragon, carrying in
his right hand a viper. He answers truly to matters present and to
come, and also of all secrets. He talketh willingly of the Creator of
Spirits, and of their fall. He saith he fell not by his own accord. He
maketh a man wonderfully learned in the liberal sciences. He
ruleth 40 Legions.

5 **BALAY**, Angel of the first heaven serving in the North on the
day of the Moon.

6 **BALIDET**, is a Minister of the King Maymon, and Angel of
the air ruling the day of Saturn, serving in the West.

7 **BABEL**, Angel of the second heaven, ruling the day of
Mercury, serving in the South.

8 **BARBAROT**, Angel of the second heaven, serving in the
East, ruling the day of Mercury.

9 **BEALPHARES**, a great King or Prince aerial.

10 **BONOHAM**, a great Duke of the fiery region.

11 **BAEL**, a King which is of the power of the East, appeareth
with three heads, the first like a toad, the second like a man, the

third like a cat, speaketh with a hoarse voice. He maketh a man go invisible. He hath under his government 66 Legions.

12 **BARBATOS**, a great Duke understandeth the singing of birds, the barking of dogs, the lowing of bullocks and the voice of all living creatures. He detecteth treasures hidden by magicians and enchanters, and was of the Order of Virtues. He knoweth what is past and to come, and reconcileth friends and powers, and governeth 30 Legions of spirits.

13 **BACIEL**, an Angel of the fourth heaven serving for the East.

14 **BACHANAEL**, an Angel of the first heaven to the West, reigning on Monday.

15 **BILET**, Minister of Arcan a King, an Angel of the air for Monday.

16 **BATHIN**, a great Duke. He is seen in the shape of a very strong man with a serpent's tail sitting on a pale horse, understanding the virtues of herbs and precious stones, transferring men suddenly from country to country and ruleth 30 Legions.

17 **BALAM**, a great and terrible King. He cometh forth with three heads, the first of a bull, the sceond of a man, the third of a ram. He hath a serpent's tail and flaming eyes riding upon a furious bear and carrying a hawk upon his fist. He speaketh with a hoarse voice answering perfectly of things past, present and to come, hath many Legions under him.

18 **BIFRONS**, at first appearance hath the similitude of a Monster, then he taketh the image of a man. He maketh one wonderful cunning in Astrology and Geometry, understands the strength and virtues of herbs, precious stones and woods, changeth and conveyeth dead bodies from place to place. He seemeth to light candles upon the sepulchres of the dead and hath under him 26 Legions.

19 **BOTIS**, a great Duke cometh in the shape of an ugly viper, and if he put on human shape he showeth great tooth and two horns, carrying a sharp sword in his hands. He giveth answers of

things present and to come, and reconcileth friends and foes, ruling 60 Legions of inferior spirits.

20 **BELIAL**, is a King, appears like a beautiful Angel sitting in a fiery chariot, speaketh fair, distributeth preferments and the favour of friends, giveth excellent familiars, ruleth 80 Legions.

21 **BERITH**, a great and terrible Duke, he cometh forth as a red soldier on a red horse with a crown on his head. He answereth truly of things past, present and to come. He turneth metals into Gold, giveth Dignities, and confirmeth them. Speaketh with a clear and subtle voice. 26 Legions are under him.

22 **BUER**, is a great President, he teaches Philosophy moral and natural, also logic and the virtue of herbs. He giveth the best familiars. He can heal all diseases, ruleth 40 Legions.

23 **BUNE**, a great Duke appeareth as a Dragon with three heads, the third whereof is like a man. He speaketh with a divine voice. He maketh the dead to change their place, and devils to assemble upon the sepulchres of the dead. He greatly enricheth a man and maketh him eloquent and wise, answereth truly to all demands and 30 Legions obey him.

24 **CAIM**, is a great President taking the form of a thrush, but when he putteth on a man's shape he answereth in burning ashes, carrying in his hands a sharp sword, giveth the understanding of all birds, lowing of bullocks, and barking of dogs. He was of the Order of Angels and ruleth thirty Legions.

25 **BILETH**, is a great King and terrible, riding upon a pale horse before whom go trumpets and all kinds of music, appeareth rough and furious, he is of the Order of Powers, hoping to return to the seventh Throne. He ruleth 85 Legions.

26 **CIMERIES**, a great Marquis and strong, ruling in the parts of Africa. He teaches the Sciences, discovereth treasures hid.

27 **CAMUEL**, the chief King of the East.

28 **CASPIEL**, the chiefest Emperor ruling in the South, he hath 200 great Dukes, and 400 lesser Dukes under him.

29 **CHOMIEL**, a great Duke under Demoriel Emperor of the North.

30 **DEAMIEL**, an Angel of the first heaven serving in the East on the day of the Moon.

31 **DAMAEL**, an Angel of the fifth heaven serving in the East on the day of Mars.

32 **DABRIEL**, an Angel of the first heaven serving in the South on the day of the Moon.

33 **DIRIEL**, a Duke under Demoriel Emperor of the North.

34 **DARQUIEL**, an Angel of the first heaven serving in the South on the day of the Moon.

35 **FRIAGNE**, an Angel of the fifth heaven ruling in the East on the day of Mars.

36 **FORCALOR**, is a great Duke. He cometh forth as a man with wings like a griffin. He killeth men and drowneth them in the waters and overturneth ships of war, commanding and ruling both winds and seas, and if the Magician biddeth him hurt no man he willingly consenteth thereto. He hath three Legions.

37 **FURCAS**, is a Knight and cometh forth in the similitude of a cruel man with a long beard and a hoary head. He sitteth on a pale horse, carrying in his hand a pale weapon. He perfectly teacheth practical philosophy, Rhetoric, Logic, Astronomy, Chiromancy, Pyromancy, and their parts. There obey him 20 Legions.

38 **GAAP**, a great President and a Prince, taketh human shape, maketh a man wonderfully knowing in philosophy and in all liberal sciences. He maketh love hatred, transferreth man most speedily into other nations, ruleth 66 Legions. He was of the Order of Powers.

39 **GEMORI**, a strong and mighty Duke appeareth like a fair woman with a Duchess's Crown, riding upon a camel, answereth all things past, present and to come, of treasures hid, procureth the love of women, hath 26 Legions.

40 **GLACIA LABOLAS**, a great President, cometh forth like a dog, hath wings like a griffin. He giveth the knowledge of arts and is the Captain of all manslayers. He understandeth things present and to come, gains the love of friends and foes, maketh a man go invisible, rules 36 Legions.

41 **GAMIGIN**, is a great Marquis and is seen in the form of a little horse. When he taketh human shape, he speaketh with a hoarse voice, disputing of all liberal sciences, bringeth to pass that the Souls which are drowned in the sea shall take airy bodies and evidently appear and answer to interrogations at the magician's commandment. He tarrieth with the exorcist till he hath accomplished his desire and hath many Legions under him.

42 **GALDEL**, an Angel of the fifth heaven ruling in the South.

43 **GABRIEL**, an Angel of the fifth heaven ruling in the East on the day of the Moon.

44 **HINIEL**, an Angel of the fifth heaven ruling in the North on the day of the Mars.

45 **MICHAEL**, the Angel of the divine Lord.

46 **MARCHOSIAS**, a Great Marquis showeth himself in the shape of a cruel she wolf with Griffin's wings and a serpent's tail. When he is in a man's shape he is an excellent fighter, answereth all questions truly. He was of the Order of Dominations. Under him are 30 Legions. He hopeth after 1200 years to come to the seventh heaven.

47 **MASGABRIEL**, a Angel of the fourth heaven, ruling in the North on the day of the Sun.

48 **MATUYEL**, a Angel of the fourth heaven, ruling in the North on the day of the Sun.

49 **MATHIEL**, a Angel of the fifth heaven, ruling in the North on the day of Mars.

50 **MITRATON**, a Angel of the second heaven, ruling in the West on the day of Mercury.

51 **MAEL**, a Angel of the first heaven, ruling in the North on the day of the Moon.

52 **MURMUR**, is a great Duke appearing in the shape of a soldier riding on a griffin with a Duke's Crown on his head. There go before him two of his ministers with great trumpets. He teacheth philosophy absolutely, constraineth souls to come before the magician to answer what he shall ask them. He was of the Order partly of Thrones and partly of Angels, and ruleth 30 Legions.

53 **NELAPA**, an Angel of the second heaven ruling in the South on the day of Mercury.

54 **OSE**, is a great President and cometh forth like a Leopard and counterfeiting to be a man. He maketh one cunning in the liberal sciences, he answereth truly of divine and secret things. He transformeth a man's shape, and bringeth a man to that madness that he thinketh himself to be that which he is not, duratque id regnum ad horam ("and it holds sway for an hour").

55 **PAIMON**, appeareth with a great cry and roaring, putting on the likeness of a man sitting on a dromedary wearing a glorious Crown, hath an effeminate countenance. There goes before him an host of men with trumpets, cymbals and all instruments. He giveth dignities, prepareth good familiars, hath the understanding of all arts. There follows him 200 Legions partly of the Order of Angels, partly of Potestates.

56 **RAHUMEL**, an Angel of the fifth heaven ruling in the North on the day of Mars.

57 **RAPHAEL**, an Angel of the third heaven ruling in the North on the day of Venus.

58 **SITRI**, is a great Prince appearing with the face of a Leopard having wings as a Griffin. When he taketh human shape he is very beautiful, he inflameth a man with woman's love, and stirreth up women to love men, being commanded he willingly destroyeth secrets of women laughing at them and mocking them to make them luxuriously naked. And there obey him sixty Legions.

59 **VALEFOR**, is a strong Duke, appears in the shape of a lion and the head of a thief. He is very familiar with them to whom he maketh himself acquainted, that he may bring them to the gallows. Ruleth ten Legions.

60 **VALAC**, is a great President, and cometh abroad with Angel's wings like a boy riding on a two headed Dragon. He perfectly answereth of treasures hidden and where serpents may be seen which he delivereth into the magician's hands void of any force or strength, and hath dominion of 30 Legions of devils.

61 **VUAL**, is a great Duke and strong. He is seen as a great and terrible Dromedary, but in human form. He soundeth in a base voice the Egyptian tongue, procureth the special love of women, and knoweth things past, present and to come, procuring the love of friends and foes. He was of the Order of Potestates and governeth 37 Legions.

The Hours Wherein the Principal Spirits May be Bound, Raised or Restrained from Doing of Hurt.

Amaymon King of the East, Corson King of the South, Zinamar King of the North, Gaap King of the West, may be bound from the third hour till noon and from the ninth hour till evening.

Marquises may be bound from the ninth hour till compline and from compline till the end of the day.

Dukes may be bound from the first hour till noon, and clear weather is to be observed.

Prelates may be bound in any hour of the day.

Knights from day dawning till the sun's rising, or from the even till the sun sets.

A President may not be bound in any hour of the day, except the King, whom he obeyeth, be invocated, nor in the shutting of the evening.

Counts or Earls may be bound in any hour of the day so it be in the woods or fields where men resort not.

Of Angels Good and Bad
Their Degrees and Offices

Lucifer and those other Angels that offended with him in ambition and pride fell not altogether into the very Abysme of Hell, though they all fell into the truest Hell which is punishment. Those which remained in the places between, was because they had not offended with so determinate an obstinacy and vehemence as the others had, and they remained also there because it was necessary and convenient for our merit, that we should have spirits for our Enemies, and in such place where they might vex us with their temptations, for which cause God permitted a great part of them to remain in the air, the earth and the water, where they shall continue till the Day of Judgement, and then they shall be all damned into the very dungeon of Hell: so that we have with them continual war: which though they be in the places aforesaid, yet are they not out of Hell in respect of torment, for their pain is all alike [See Aquinas, Quest. 64. Ar. 4]. The Difference of the Degrees of spirits is rehearsed by Gaudentius Merula taking the same out of Psellius who maketh Six kinds or degrees of spirits between heaven and hell. The first are those that remained in the highest Region of the Air, he calleth Angels of fire because they are near unto that region and perchance within it. The second kind, saith he, is from the middle region of the air downwards towards the earth. The third on the Earth itself. The fourth in the waters. The fifth in the Caves and hollow vaults of the earth. The sixth in the very dungeon and abysme of hell. In such sort, that they are as it were interlinked one with another, but all these spirits have duties and offices of divers sorts. For the chiefest grief and pain of the first which were those that had least offended, seeing themselves so near Heaven, is the Contemplation: that through their wickedness they have left so great a beatitude (though this be general to them all), and those are nothing so harmful as the others are. For those which are in the middle of the region of the air, and those that are under them nearer the Earth, are those which sometimes, out of the ordinary operation of nature, do move the winds with greater fury than they are accustomed and do out of season congeal the clouds causing it to thunder, lighten, hail and to destroy the grass, corn, vines and fruits of the Earth, and these are they whose help the Necromancers do often use in their devilish operations. An example to this purpose I find in *Malleus Malleficarum:* the Commissioners having apprehended certain sorceresses, willed one of them to show that she could do, assuring her life on condition that from hence forward, she should no more offend in the like. Whereupon, going out of the fields in presence of the Commissioners and others, she made a pit in the ground with her hands making her water into the same, which being done she stirred around the urine with one of her fingers, out of the which by little and little after she had made certain characters and mumbled a few words, there arose a vapour which ascending upwards like a smoke, began to thicken of itself in the midst of the Region of the air, gathering and making there a black fearful cloud, which cast out so many thunders and lightnings that it seemed to be a thing hellish and Infernal. The woman remaining all this while still, asked the Commissioners where they would have that cloud to discharge a great quantity of stones, they pointing her to a certain place where it could do no hurt at all, the cloud of a sudden began to move itself with a great furious blustering of winds and in short space coming over the place appointed, discharged a great number of stones like a violent shower directly within the compass thereof. And in this sort may the witches and Necromancers make many such like things through the help of these spirits.

But now to declare the office and function of a third kind of spirits being on the earth whose principal office and function is to persecute men and to tempt and allure men to sin, and thereby to work their damnation, envying that those places that they once enjoyed in heaven, should be possessed and replenished with men, see here the Devil's malice which proceedeth only of envy. These spirits vex, deceive, entice us sleeping and waking. To defend us from their temptations we have an Angel Guardian to direct and guard us, and we have at our left hand an ill spirit which still solicits and allures us to sin. Their power is restrained that they cannot put in execution the full puissance of their malicious desires without the permission of God.

A strange chance happened to a boy in the city of Astorges. A man of good quality and learning there had two sons, the one being about twelve or thirteen years old had by some fault so offended his mother that in a rage she cursed him with detestable Maledictions betaking him to the Devils of Hell, and wishing that they would fetch him out of her presence. This was about ten at night, being very dark; the foolish woman continuing her curses so long, till at last the boy, through fear went out into a little court behind the house, out of which he suddenly vanished, and though they diligently searched round the house they could be no means find him, at which they exceedingly wondered, for both the doors of the house were locked, and round the house they searched but could find no way for his going out. About two hours after, they heard in a chamber above their heads a very great noise, and withal the young boy groaning with extreme anguish and grief. They presently going up and opening the chamber door which they found also fast locked, they perceived the silly boy groveling on the ground in a most pitiful manner, for besides his garments rent to pieces, his face and hands and in a manner his whole body scratched and grated as if he had been drawn through briars and thorns, and he was so disfigured and dismayed, that he came not all that night to himself. In the meantime, his parents caused him to be dressed and cured, omitting nothing to the recovery of his health. The next day, after his senses were somewhat comforted, and he began to recover his judgement, they asked him by what means this accident had happened to him. To whom he made answer, that as he stood in the court there came unto him certain men of exceeding great stature, grim in countenance and in gesture loathsome and horrible, who presently without speaking any word hoisted him up into the air and carried him away with such swiftness, that it was not possible to his seeming for any bird in the world to fly so fast; and at last lighting down amongst certain mountains full of bushes and briars, they trailed him through the thickest part of them from one side to another, with intention to kill, he had at last the grace and memory to commend himself unto God beseeching Him to help and assist him: at which very instant they turned back with him through the air, and put him in a little window which was there in the chamber, where when they had left him they vanished away. The boy lived many years after but remained ever after deaf and dull conceited, never recovering his former quickness and vivacity of spirit, taking continually exceeding grief when any man talked to him of this matter.

The fourth kind of Spirits are those which are in the water as well the Sea as floods, rivers and lakes. These never cease to raise damps and storms persecuting those which sail, putting them in great dangers through violent and raging tempests, procuring to destroy and drown the ships also through the aid of monstrous rocks and shallows which are in the sea. Overturning the boats that are in the rivers, and causing those that swim to entangle themselves in sedges or woods, or bringing them into some pits or holes where they cannot get out, and by all means possible persecute and molest them so far as the limitation of their power extendeth.

The fifth kind of Spirits are those which are in the caves and vaults of the Earth, where they lie in wait to entrap those that dig in mines and wells and other works underground, whose death and destruction they covet and procure as much as they may. These cause the motions and tremblings of the earth through the aid of the Winds which are there enclosed, whereby whole cities are often in danger to be swallowed up, especially those which are built near the Sea. Whole mountains are hereby thrown down, infinite people destroyed; sometimes the sea hereby breaketh into the land wasting and destroying whatever it findeth before it.

The sixth and last kind of Spirits are those who are in the Abysme and place called Hell, whose principal and proper office is, besides the pains which they endure, to torment the damned souls. This place, saith Job, hath no order at all but continual fear, horror and amazement.

Apuleius, who made himself so well acquainted with Spirits of all sorts, writeth that there is a kind of Spirits who are always free from the strings and bonds of the body, of which number is sleep and love whom he termeth Spirits; whereby he seemeth to confess, that there are others which have bodies, and so thinketh St. Basil, who attributeth bodies not only to these spirits but also to the Angels: Psellius is of the same opinion.

It is the general opinion of all the fathers and doctors of the Church as well ancient as modern, that the Angels when it is necessary do fashion and make unto themselves visible bodies, for the effects which they pretend, as we find in many places of the holy Scriptures: whether it be of air thickened, or fire, or of earth, it maketh no matter; but that so it is — see what is written of the three Angels that came to the house of Abraham in the likeness of three beautiful young men. And the Angel Gabriel appeared to the glorious Virgin in a most goodly form and figure when he brought her the Salutation. The self same is permitted to devils in their operations, whose bodies though we call phantastical, because they vanish quickly away, yet they verily are visible bodies formed of such substance as I said before, but the same is so fine and delicate that it straight dissolveth and vanisheth. To say something of a Phantasm which hath his beginning in the phantasy, which is a virtue in man called by another name Imaginative, and because this virtue being moved, worketh in such sort, that it causeth in itself the things feigned and imagined to seem present, though in truth they are not. We say also, that the things which vanish away so soon as we have seen them are phantasies, seeming to us that we deceive ourselves, and that we saw them not, but that they were only represented in our fancy. But this is in such sort that sometimes we truly see them indeed, and other times our Imagination and fancy so present them to our view, that they deceive us, and we understand not whether they were things seen or imagined, and therefore comes it, that we call the things which we really see 'Visions', and others which are represented to the phantasy 'Fancies'.

Of Incubi and Succubi

Devils are Incubi and Succubi taking oftentimes to that end the shape and likeness, sometimes of men, sometimes of women, and commit the greatest abominations that may be, so that jointly they may procure and cause men to commit it with them. Coelius Rodiginus saith that there was in Greece a man called Marcus who had great familiarity with Devils, for which cause he lived always solitary conversing little with other men. This man uttered many of the Devil's secrets, of which this of ye Incubi and Succubi was one, and many others that for their filthiness and abomination are not to be spoken of; but according to his confession, all the Devils do not use this execrable offence, but those only who are near unto us, and do form their bodies of a gross substance, as of water or earth. St. Augustine saith, that the Satyrs and Fauns were thought of some to be Incubi, because they were so luxurious. Hence many took occasion to authorise that for truth which is reported of Merlin that he was begotten of a Devil, but this is better said than affirmed, for whether it be or not, God only knoweth.

In the Diocese of Bamberg there was a virgin that brought forth a Son and remained a true virgin afterwards, for whilst the maid slept the Daemon defiled her, she was wholly ignorant of the deceit upon examination of honest Matrons, many advised her to marry, that she might bring forth without danger of her life, but she resolved to keep her vow of virginity though her death might follow. When her time was come she was delivered of a birth, and lived many years after in great devotion.

The Power and Authority that Necromancers and Witches Have Over the Devil

They constrain the Devils and make them perforce obey and accomplish their commands, carrying them bound and enclosed in rings, boxes and little Vials, applying their helps to such as far as they please, and such Devils they commonly call Familiars. The Art of Necromancy was used in old time by faithful and unfaithful and in our days by divers. This Art may be exercised in two sorts. The first is Natural, which may be wrought through things, whose virtue and property is natural to do them, as herbs, plants and stones, and other things as the planets and heavenly influences, and this Art is lawful and may be used and practiced of those that can attain to this knowledge of their hidden properties. Aquinas, in his book, *De Ente et Essentia*, alleged that Abel the son of Adam made a book of all the virtues and properties of the planets foreknowing that the world should perish through the general flood, he enclosed so cunningly in a stone that the waters could not come to corrupt the same, whereby it might be preserved and known to all people. This stone was found by Hermes Trismegistus, who breaking it, and finding the book therein enclosed, profited wonderfully by applying the contents thereof to his use; which Book, coming afterwards into the hand of St. Thomas, he did therewith many great experiences, one was, that being sick and troubled with the noise of beasts and carriages that passed through the street, remedied that trouble by making an Image as the book proscribed him, which being buried in the street none of all the beasts had power to pass thereby, but coming thither stayed or went backwards, nor could by any man be constrained to do the contrary. He also telleth of a certain friend of his, who by the same book, made an Image, and putting it into a fountain, it caused all such vessels as touched the water thereof to break presently, which came by observation of certain hours and points in working of those Images, of which they took great account and heed, to the end that the planets might the better use their influence in working those things which seemed supernatural. The use of all this is so lawful that nothing can be said to the contrary.

The other kind of Necromancy or Art of Magic, is that which is used and practised through the help and favour of the Devil, which hath been long time exercised in the world. Of this the Holy Scriptures testify, speaking of the Magicians of Pharoah, who contended with Moses and Aaron, as in the New Testament in the Acts making mention of Simon Magus rebuked by St. Peter, and besides you must understand that the Devils may be forced and constrained by the good Angels, and this is because of the Grace which the one lost, and the other as yet retains.

None can use or exercise this Art of Necromancy unless he first make a secret Agreement or express Covenant with the Devil, and such Devils with whom they deal in those Covenants are not of the common sort but of a higher and superior condition, for amongst themselves they do observe their orders and degrees of superiority, as Franciscus de Victoria asserts, and this is for the better use of their wickedness, and so saith Aquinas.

Some Devils are preferred as principals to command the rest, and the inferior Devils are subject unto those, which are of mighty force to execute their wickedness. And therefore the Jews said unto Christ, that he wrought his Miracles in the name of Beelzebub, the Prince of Devils, so that the Necromancer and Magicians that are confederated with the Princes and Captains of the Infernal army, have always the lesser and inferior Devils in a readiness at Commandment to do their will and pleasure, being thereunto constrained by those of the higher dignity and condition.

It is the opinion of St. Augustine and Aquinas that the Devils are not kept bound and enclosed in rings, boxes or Vials. The Devils may make them believe so with whom they deal, for they are where and in what place, and when they list themselves, and how far soever they be off, yet at such time as they are called, or their presence required, they come in at that instant to make answer to those which holding them for familiars, and thinking surely that they carry them always present with them, demand or ask anything of them, who are greatly abused and deceived in presuming that they are able to hold them forcibly at their Commandment, because it proceedeth not through the words of the Necromancer, but through the might and authority of the higher Spirits and

Devils which as Captains govern and Command them. Yea, and sometime constraining them to remain bound indeed, when they have any notable exploit in hand, but also for the most part they have them always at liberty

Of Spirits Called Hobgoblins or Robin Goodfellows

These kinds of Spirits are more familiar and domestical than the others, and for some causes to us unknown, abide in one place more than in another, so that some never almost depart from some particular houses, as though they were their proper Mansions, making in them sundry noises, rumours, mockeries, gawds and jests, without doing any harm at all, and some have heard them play on Gitterns and Jews harps, and ring bells and make answer to those that call them, and speak with certain signs, laughters and merry gestures, so that those of the house come at last to be so familiar, and well acquainted with them that they fear them not at all. But in truth, if they had free power to put in execution their malicious desire, we should find these pranks of theirs not to be jests, but earnest indeed, tending to the destruction both of our body and soul, but their power is so restrained and tied that they can pass no further than to jests and gawds, and if they do any harm at all it is certainly very little as by experience has been found.

Of the Orders of Wicked Demons
and of their Fall and their Divers Natures

These wicked Demons are divided into nine degrees or Orders, as the good Angels are divided into nine Orders or Hierarchies.

1 Pseudothei

The first Order of Demons are called Pseudothei or false gods who usurp God's name, would be worshipped as Gods, have adoration and sacrifice made to them, as that Demon said to Christ—if thou wilt fall down and worship me, all shall be thine. And the Prince of these Demons is Beelzebub, that is an old God, he said I shall ascend above the height of the clouds and be like the Most High.

2 Spiritus Mendaciorum

After these follow the spirits of Lying, of which kind was he that was a lying spirit in the mouths of Ahab's prophets. And their Prince is that spirit Python, from whom Apollo Pythius was called, and that pythonic woman with Samuel, and that other woman in the Gospels that had a python in her belly. This kind of Demon deceives by their Oracles, divinations and predictions.

3 Vasa Iniquitatis

In the third Order are the Vessels of Iniquity, which are called the Vessels of Anger. These are the inventors of mischiefs and of all wicked Arts. Plato mentions one of these wicked Demons that was called Theutus who taught plays, dice and cards; from these proceed all wickedness, malice and deformity.

In Genesis, Jacob called Symeon and Levi 'Vessels of Iniquity', in their dwellings with the Psalmist 'Vessels of Death', Isaiah called them 'Vessels of Fury', and Jeremiah 'Vessels of Anger', and Ezekiel 'Vessels of Killing and Destruction'. And the Prince of them is Belial, which is interpreted—without an yoke, or disobedient, a prevaricator and Apostate; of whom Paul saith to the Corinthians—What Convention of Christ with Belial.

4 Ultores Scelorum

The Revengers of Wickedness, and their Prince is Asmodeus, that is, doing Judgement.

5 Praestigiatores

The Praestigiators come into the fifth Order, who imitate Miracles, and serve the Caco-magi and Malefics, and seduce people in their miracles as the Serpent seduced Eve, and their Prince is Sathan, who seduces the whole world.

6 Aeriae Potestates

The Aerial Powers offer themselves in the sixth Order, who mix themselves with thunders and lightnings, corrupting the Air bringing pestilence and other evils, of which number are the four Angels in the Apocalypse to whom it was given to hurt the Earth and Sea, holding the four Winds from the four Corners of the Earth. And their Prince is called Merizim. This is a South Demon, a raging and furious Demon in the South whom Paul calls in the Ephesians, a Prince of the power of the air and a spirit which works in the Children of Disobedience.

7 Furiae

The seventh Mansion the Furies hold — the Sowers of Mischief and discord, wars, and destruction, whose Prince in the Apocalypse is called in Greek Apollyon, in Hebrew Abaddon, that is, destroying and laying waste.

8 Criminatores

In the eighth place stand the Criminators or Accusers, whose Prince is Astaroth, that is, an Explorator in Greek. He is called Diabolus, that is a Criminator or Calumniator, who in the Apocalypse is called an Accuser of the Brethren day and night before the face of God.

9 Tentatores Maligenii

The last place hold the Tempters, who we call the bad Genii and their Prince is Mammon, who is interpreted Coveteousness. But these bad Demons do unanimously infect this lower world, and therefore are called Diaboli.

And it is an opinion that these Apostate Angels or Devils shall persuade very many Angels to decline with him, who are now called his Angels, but St. Basil thinks not that they are all condemned and purposively wicked, but that they should be appointed from the beginning to be the Carnificina for souls offending. Other divines say that no Demons were created wicked but were cast down from the Heavens from the Orders of good Angels, for their prevarication, as all Hebrew divines, Assyrian, Arabian and Egyptian do confirm. Phererides the Syrian describes the fall of Demons, and Ophin, that is a Serpent Demoniac, that was the head of the rebellious army. But those Demons thrown down into this valley of Misery, being near us do wander up and down in this dark air. Others inhabit lakes, rivers and seas, others terrify the Earth and earthly things, and invade the diggers of wells and metals. They provoke the gapings of the Earth and shake the foundations of mountains, neither do they vex men only but living creatures. Others sometimes putting on a gigantic body very tall, and then appear very small like pigmies turning themselves into diverse figures, trouble men with vain terror; others study lies and blasphemies, as in Kings 3, 22 — "I will be a lying spirit in the mouth of all Ahab's prophets."

But the worst sort of Demons are those who molest men in their journeys rushing upon them that pass along, rejoice in wars and effusion of blood and afflict men with sore insults. In the Psalms they are called asps, basilisks, lions, dragons. In the Gospel called Scorpion and Mammon, the Prince of this world and Rector of darkness whose Prince is Beelzebub. Porphyry calls him Serapis and the Greeks Pluto.

Origen pleaded for the Demons admission into favour. Many of the lapsed Angels may hope to be saved, and bring this argument out of the Gospel that Christ heard the prayers of Demons and suffered them to go into the herd of swine. Psalm 72, the Ethiopians shall fall down before him, and his enemies shall lick the dust, but according to the Hebrews, verily it runs thus. Before him the inhabitants of solitude shall bend their knees, that is, the aerial spirits shall worship him as the Cabalists do assert, and his enemies shall lick the dust, which they expound of Zazel and his army, of whom it is read in Genesis — "Thou shalt eat dust all the days of thy life." Hence the Cabalists think that some demons may be saved and it was the opinion of Origen.

Of the Bodies of Demons

There are great differences among Divines and Philosophers. Aquinas affirms that all the Angels as well as wicked demons are incorporeal, but sometimes they assume bodies which they presently put off. Dionysius in his Divine Names affirms that the Angels are without bodies.

Augustine upon Genesis saith that Demons are said to be airy as well as fiery animals, neither are they loosed by death because there prevails in them the Element to act rather than to suffer, and further saith that all Angels from the beginning of their Creation had aerial bodies formed from the pure and more superior part of the air fit for action not passion, and these bodies were preserved after confirmation by the good Angels, but by the bad Angels were changed into the quality of grosser air that they might suffer by fire.

The great Basil doth not only attribute bodies to Demons but also to pure Angels, as certain small aerial and pure spirits. And Gregory Nazianzene agrees to this, also Apuleius that all demons have bodies as you may read of Socrates Daemon. Psellus the Platonic and Christian held that demons by nature could not be without a body, as bodies of shadows and subject to passion, as if smitten should be more sorrowful, and if burnt should turn to ashes, which was proved true in Tuscia. According to the mixture of the Elements among themselves, so are the different kinds of the bodies of demons, which will require a large discourse if all objections to the contrary are answered.

Divines are of the opinion that all wicked demons are of that nature that they equally hate God as well as man, but divine providence hath ordered good demons more pure and near to us to watch over us and daily help us, and that they may drive away and bind those bad demons that they may not hurt us as they would do. You may read in Tobit of Raphael that bound Asmodeus a Demon in the desert of the Upper Egypt.

Clavis Enochi Tabularum
et Artis Magicae secundum Cardanum, Iamblichus, Alstedium, et Dee et Alios authores.

Some deny an immaterial being, and that nothing can be sine materia, and removing corporeal matters out of this world there will still remain space and distance in which this very matter, while it was there, was accustomed to lie, and this distant space cannot but be something, and yet not corporeal, because neither corruptible, impenetrable nor tangible, it must of necessity be a substance incorporeal, necessarily and eternally existent of itself, which the clear Idea of a being absolutely perfect will more fully and punctually inform us to be the self subsisting God or Immaterial Being.

Of Astromantic and Geomantic Gamahes

See Paracelsus Tom. 2. Lib. 4. *De Causis Morborum Invisibilium.*

The Ghosts of dead men called Evestia, which are often seen to appear in churchyards, are natural effects being only the forms of the bodies which are buried in those places, or their outward shapes or figures and not the souls of these men, or any such like apparition caused by evil spirits as the common opinion is. The Ancients thought that these Ghosts were the good and evil Genii which attended always upon armies, but they are to be excused seeing they know not how to give any other reason of these apparitions.

It is most certain that in armies where there are great numbers, many die, you shall see some such Ghosts very often (especially after a battle) which are the Genii of the Air.

From whence these questions may arise:

Firstly, whether or no we may by these explain all the visions that are mentioned by writers.

Secondly, whether those wonderful effects which we attribute to Daemons or Spirits may proceed from these figures or not.

Thirdly, whether they have any power or not? And if it be granted they have any, Paracelsus is of opinion their Mummy hath in it all virtues of plants, stones, etc., and that it hath in it an occult Magnetic virtue which draws men to the sepulchres of those whom they account to have been holy men, whereby the virtue of the same Mummy there, are those effects wrought which we call miracles; which are observed to be much more frequent in the summer, than in any other season of the year, by reason of the heat of the Sun, which awakens and excites the humour, that is in the Mummy.

Fourthly, whether or no these wonderful forms which proceed

from the blood, the bones or the ashes of dead bodies, may serve for an undeniable argument of the Resurrection, a thing unknown to most of the Philosophers.

Fifthly, whether after they are raised up they can in any thing be serviceable unto us?

And sixthly, whether by their means we may be naturally able to attain to the knowledge of diverse secrets which are unknown to us. Though the body be reduced to ashes yet the figure is not thereby destroyed.

Of Telesmes (Talismans)

They are called in Hebrew מֵגֶן i.e. a Scutcheon or Shield; in Chaldaic, Egyptian or Persian צַלְמָיָא i.e. Tsilmonia, it signifies a figure or Image; in Arabic תַלְצְמָם Talitsman or צלמם Tsaliman; and in Greek ΣΤΟΙΧΕΙΑ. Maghon signifies properly any piece of paper marked or noted with certain characters drawn from the Tetragrammaton, instead of a buckler or shield of defense against diseases, lightnings or tempests. Read Salmasius and Scaliger.

These figures are unlike those images of wax which sorcerers were of old want to baptise in the name of Beelzebub, these are abominations. But now I will declare what natural power these images may have which are made under certain constellations, banishing from hence all operations of Demons or spirits and all superstitious powers whatsoever.

I shall prove the power of figures and Images three ways: first, by the influence of the stars; second, by the power of resemblance; and thirdly, by experience.

Authentic historiographers affirm that there have been seen some of these Telesmes, Telesmanical, Telesmatical (which is all one), or figures that have been bitten by serpents, scorpions, mad dogs and diverse other mischances. The ancient Arabians as Almansor, Messahala, Zahel, Albohazen, Haly, Rhodoam, Albategnius, Homar, Zachdir, Hahamed and Serapion, give many examples of this kind, which gave Haly occasion to conclude that—"Utilem Serpentis Imaginem effici posse, quando Luna Serpentem coelestem subit aut foeliciter aspicit: Similiter Scorpionis effigium efficarem, quando Scorpii signum Luna ingreditur," (The usefulness of the image of the Serpent is made effective when the Moon is increasing and has a favourable aspect to the celestial Sign or Constellation of the Serpent, similarly, the effigy of the Scorpion is made effective when the Moon enters the sign of Scorpio). Haly experimented this doctrine in Egypt. He had there in his hand one of these Images of a Scorpion which did cure those that were stung by this venomous beast; and it was engraved on a Bezar stone.

Eugenius, besides an infinite number of rarities which he

reports of Egypt, says that when they were sometimes digging in the Bridge at Apamia, there was found a piece of Copper whereon was to be seen the figure of a Rat, of a serpent and of a fire, which being afterwards neglected as peradventure either broken to pieces or in some way or other spoiled, there was observed in a very short time after a great number of serpents and rats to haunt the city, and they do greatly annoy it still; and we cannot without grief call to mind the many great losses the City hath from that time endured by fire: all which sad accidents were never heard of before the taking up of this strange Plate of Copper.

Camerarius reports Lib. 2, Cap. 20, that after that Mahomet the Second possessed himself of Constantinople, the breaking of the lower jaw of a brazen serpent was the cause of the increasing of serpents in those parts.

And by means of these Telesmes, learned men of the ages past have often chased away insects out of their cities and fields as Gnats, Locusts and Caterpillars. See the *Chiliads* of John Tzetzes, who lived *circa annum* 1160, where the Greek author (who lived about the time of that excellent historian Anna Comnena, daughter to the Emperor Elexius Comnenus) reports that Apollonius by making a Telesman of a stork, kept those troublesome birds from coming into Constantinople; and by another Telesman he drove away all the Gnats out of Antioch—see Ptolomy's *Centriloquium* and the *Commentary of Abregefer.*

The first Gods of the Latins called Averrunci or Dii Tutelares were no more than these Telesmanical figures or images. Some historians affirm that they made some of these Tutelar gods under certain Constellations, but the poison of Idolatry having infected the best of sciences was the cause that these images being afterwards taken for Gods, the true and legitimate manner of making them was smothered. They were wont also to set up some of these Telesmes upon the prow of their ships to preserve them from shipwreck, and this done naturally too; seeing that a Telesman may be made under the sign Pisces, that may for some certain time render the waters calm and free from tempests. The Greeks (as Hesychi Herodotus) called these figures set up in ships ΠΑΙΑΙΧΟΥΣ [?], a word no doubt borrowed from the Hebrew פסחוים

Pitochim which signifies Coelatura, and therefore the Chaldaic
paraphrase renders it by this our צַלְמֵיָּא Tsilmenaia. These figures
were not at all of any human form but of some Celestial figure or
other which demonstrates that they were real Telesmans. Nevertheless, the mariners had also their statues of some deity or other,
as of Mars, Apollo, Venus, Mercury and the like, which they placed
at the poop or hinder parts of their ships as Virgil says—"Aurato ful-
gebat Apolline puppis." Which made the poets feign that Jupiter
stole away Europa under the shape of a bull, because the ship of the
Cretians who stole her away had for its Telesman the figure of the
celestial Taurus, and for its deity a statue of Jupiter.

This custom of mariners setting up these Telesmans or images
in their vessels against shipwreck, is so ancient, that they say that
among those that came with Aeneas from Troy, there was one that
had the figure of two Lions; that the Gadarenes had one with the
image of a horse, and that the ship of Alexandria which St. Paul
sailed in had the images of Castor and Pollux, or according to the
Arabians, the Gemini graved on it; and that which carried Hypo-
crates when he took his journey to Abdera for the curing of
Democritus, bore the figure of the Sun. Now all these Telesmans
were not made so much for the avoiding of shipwreck only, as for
the turning away of some other disasterous accidents or the
procuring of some good fortune. And from this practice of the
ancients have the Christians taken example, though in a Christian
way, of having images in their vessels and picturing in them the
Saints whose names they bear.

These Telesmans were not set up in cities and ships only, but
also in the plain open fields too, and it may be that that Stone so
much famed among the Turks, which they call Bractan and is set
up in Mecca, being 4 foot long and 2 foot broad as Suidas reports,
was only a Telesman. For otherwise we must even content ourselves with Turkish fables, and believe that it would never have
been so highly prized by them, but for that it served instead of a bed
to Abraham when he had knowledge of his maid Hagar. Others say
that the reason why the Turks have this stone in so much veneration is because that Abraham tied his Camel to it when he went up
to the Mountain to sacrifice his son as Euthymius Zigabenus

affirms. Others say it was erected in memory of a certain holy woman who was taken up into heaven and afterwards honoured upon Earth as a Goddess, having very charitably entertained the Angels Arot and Marot. The figure of Venus was engraven on this stone with a Crescent which makes me believe that it was a Telesman of this planet, which M. Selden the great antiquary saith was anciently taken through all Asia for the Moon, which makes them venerate Friday as much as we do Sunday, in memory of Venus, which all the Asians worshipped and adorned their houses and tops of their Temples with little crescents, as ours are with crosses. This stone was placed in the open fields and not within any temple. By its virtue it drove away all venomous beasts, and made all the neighbouring fields both happy and fruitful, but the nature of this Telesman lasted but for a certain time as Albertus Magnus assures us.

Albinus Villanovensis shows us how to make a Telesman for to cure the tertian and quatran ague, the pain of the nerves, ventricles and privy parts. Grave the image of a scorpion upon a piece of Gold or Silver when the Sun is in his proper house and the Moon in Capricorn, and while you are graving it you must say these words— Exurge Domine gloria mea, Exurge Psalterium et Cithara, Exurgam diluculo—and then rehearse this Psalm—Miserere mei Deus miserere mei, quia in te confidit anima mea.

Cardinal Capetan lays down this true and powerful conclusion in favour of Telesmanical figures. "Figura licet non sit ipsum principium operationis est tamen con principium." He proves the antecedent, "quia in artificium instrumentis efficit figura, ut ille sic vel sit operentur; tuam quia ferrum latum super aquas fertur quod si in formam aliam contrahas demergetur.

Of the Telesmatical Images of the faces and of those images which are within the Zodiac.

There are besides in the Zodiac 36 images according to the number of the faces, of the which (as Porphyry saith) Teurer the Babylonian long since wrote, who was an eminent and ancient mathematician after whom the Arabians also wrote of these things.

Of Telesmes and How to Make Them

It was a Rule the trembling Heathen went by to undertake nothing inauspicate without some ominous performance, still obtaining their end by what dark and secret ways of co-operation soever brought to pass as undiscovered to themselves as us.

Of the foundation of Antioch read the Arabian history of Abdilphaker. When King Antiochus laid the foundation, it happened that whatsoever the workmen dug up by day, was again thrown in by night, and they were affrighted from the work by a dreadful apparition; the King called for the Astrologers and Wise Men, who after sacrifice rightly performed, discovered an appearance of Almarick or Mars. It was agreed, therefore, that a magnificent Temple should be erected to his name and his statue there set up, and that the foundation of the City should be laid under his Ascendant. Also an anniversary of three days festival was instituted, etc. These things continued until the manifestation of Jesus the Son of Mary.

In giving judgments of the Accidents of a City, take knowledge of the Sun and Moon's place in the Zodiac which they had at the laying of the foundation, but especially of the Ascendant as the most principal Angel: and the figures of Geomancy. According to these rules, Taricus Firmicus cast the nativity of Rome, and Vectius Valens an Astrologer of Antioch that of Constantinople, the figure whereof is extant in a Greek Manuscript in the Vatican. The Horoscope was Cancer ♋ and the Astrologer judged by the appearance that the city should stand 702 years. In the Tables of Alkas, Constantinople is set up under Libra ♎. In Ben Isaac's *Geography* under Taurus ♉, Amissio or ♀ in ♉.

The founders of old at the building of their principal Cities, Castles or the like, cause the Astrologers to find out a lucky position of the heavens under which the first stone might be laid. The part of fortune found out in the first figure was made the Ascendant of another. The first judged of the livelihood and duration. The second of the outward glory and fortune of the City under the influence of this latter configuration, they erected a figure of brass into which this fortune and genius of the City was to be called by art. Thus spirited with this secret power it was disposed of in some eminent or recessful place of the City, and looked upon as that thing which was only concerned in the fortune and fatality of all.

Clavis Magicae
seu Enochi Tabularum Explanatio

Triplex Mundus — Elementalis, Coelestis, Intellectualis

Hebraica lingua est pernecessaria Artem Magicam investigare

Omnis Litera cum vocali sonum integrum edit unde et Consona dicitur.

Litera sunt viginti dua omnes Consona

1 a	א	Aleph	40 m	מ	Mem
2 b	ב	Beth	50 n	נ	Nun
3 g	ג	Gimel	60 s	ס	Samech
4 d	ד	Daleth	70 gn	ע	Gnaym
5 h	ה	He	80 p	פ	Pe
6 u	ו	Vau	90 tz	צ	Tzade
7 z	ז	Zajn	100 k	ק	Koph
8 ch	ח	Cheth	200 r	ר	Rosch
9 t	ט	Teth	300 s	ש	Schin
10 i	י	Jod	400 th	ת	Thau.
20 c	כ	Caph			
30 l	ל	Lamed			

Litera finales sunt quinque quae in fine vocum aliter scribuntur, unde litera finales vocantur: nempe ך ם ן ף ץ

ך ם ן ף ץ
tzade pe nun mem caph

ש est s.
שׁ est sch.

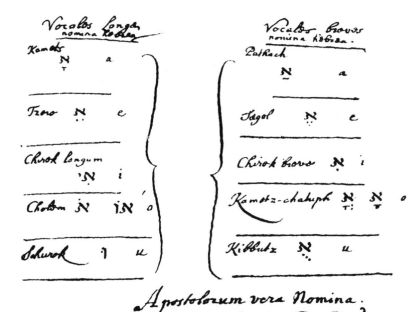

Vocales longæ nomina Hebræa

Kamats א a

Tzere א e

Chirok longum אי i

Cholem א וא o

Schurok ו u

Vocales breves nomina Hebræa.

Pathach א a

Segol א e

Chirok breve א i

Kamotz-chatuph א א o

Kibbutz א u

Apostolorum vera Nomina.

1. שמעון . כבפי , Symeon Hacaphi, hic est Petrus.

2. אלקוזי Abuzi, quem vocamus Andream.

3. יעק כה Jahacobah, hic est Jacobus major.

4. פוליפוש Polipos, quem nuncupamus Philippum

5. ברכיה Barachiah, hic est Bartholomaus.

6. יוהנה Johanah, quem pronunciamus Johannem

7. תמני Thamni, hunc pronunciamus Thomam.

8. מדון Medon, pro quo dicimus Mattheum.

9. יעקב Jahacob, hic est Jacobus.

10. חטיפא Catypha hic est Thadaus.

11. שמאם Samam qui est Symon Chananaus

12. מתתיה Matattiah qui dicitur Mathias.

Of the Images of the Fixed Behenian Stars

According to Hermes Trismegistus under the head of Algol they made an Image whose figure was the head of a man with a bloody neck which bestoweth good success to petitions and maketh him who carried it bold and magnanimous and preserveth the members of the body sound, it helpeth against witchcraft.

Under the Constellation of Pleiades they made the Image of a little virgin or the figure of a Lamp. It is reported to increase the light of the eyes, to assemble spirits, to raise winds to reveal secrets and hidden things.

Under Aldebaran they made an Image after the likeness of God or of a flying man, it giveth riches and honour.

Under the Goat they made an Image, the figure of which was as it were a man willing to make himself merry with musical instruments, it maketh him who carried it honoured and exalted before Kings and Princes.

Under the Greater Dog star they made the Image of a Hound and a little Virgin. It bestoweth honour and favour of men and aerial spirits, reconcileth Princes and other men.

Under the Lesser Dog star they made the Image of a Cock. It conferreth the favour of spirits and men, giveth power against witchcraft and preserveth health.

Under the heart of Leo they made the Image of a Lion or Cat. It rendereth a man temperate, appeaseth wrath and giveth favour.

Under the Tail of Ursa Major they made the Image of a pensive man, of a bull, or of a calf. It availeth against incantations and maketh him who carried it secure in his travels.

Under the wings of Corvus ⟩⟩ᵒᵈ they made the Image of a Raven or Snake or of a black man clothed. This maketh a man bold, courageous, a back biter, causeth naughty dreams, also it giveth the power of driving away evil spirits and of gathering them together.

Under the Spike ⟩⟨ (Spica ♍) they made the Image of a bird, or of a man beladen with merchandise. It conferreth riches and maketh one overcome contentions, it taketh away scarcity and mischief.

Under Alchameth ⟩⟨⟩ they made the Image of a horse or wolf, or the figure of a man dancing. It is good against fevers, it astringeth and retaineth the blood.

Under Elphrya or Elpheia ⟩⟨⟩ they made the Image of a Hen, or of a man crowned and advanced. It bestoweth the good will and love of men and giveth chastity.

Under the Heart of Scorpio ⟩⟨⟩ they made the Image of a man armed, and with a coat of mail, or the figure of a scorpion. It giveth understanding and memory, it maketh a good colour, and aideth against evil spirits, and driveth them away and bindeth them.

Under the Vulture ⟩⟨⟩ they made the Image of a vulture or hen, or of a traveller. It maketh a man magnanimous and proud, it giveth power over Devils and beasts.

Under the Tail of Capricorn ⟩⟨⟩ they made the Image of a heart or goat, or of an angry man. It bestoweth prosperity and increaseth wrath.

Theophrastus Paracelsus wrote a Book called *Archidoxes*, wherein he gives the true direction how to make certain Images on certain metals and otherwise how the metal must be spermatic and callow before it can receive the Astral Agent. These figures are not made according to the similitude of Celestial figures, but according to the similitude of that which the mind of the worker desires, being guided by an admirable Genius. These figures answer several uses, to procure love, to cure several distempers, etc. Albertus Magnus in his Speculo, as also Weckerus, a German, have written a large volume of the use and virtues of these Images or Sigils.

They use the Images being made diversely according to the virtues thereof. Sometimes they hang them in a chimney over the smoke, or upon a tree that they be moved by the wind, sometimes with the head upwards and sometimes downwards, sometimes they put them into hot water, or into the fire. For they say, as the workers of the Images do affect the Images itself, so doth it bring the like passions upon those to whom it was ascribed, as the minds of the Operator hath dictated it. As Nectanabus the Magician made Images of wax representing ships after that manner and art, that when he drowned those images in water that the ships of the Enemies were in like manner drowned in the Sea and hazarded.

The Alphabet of Angels
or the Writing and Language of Heaven

God and Spirits can speak any language, yet many doubt whether Angels or Genii, since they be pure spirits, use any vocal speech or tongue amongst themselves.

The Platonists say that Socrates perceived his Genius by sense indeed; but not of this body but by the sense of the ethereal body concealed in this. After which manner Averroes believes the Angels were wont to be heard and seen by the prophets. That instrument, whatsoever, the virtue be, by which one spirit makes known to another spirit what things are in his mind, is called by the Apostle St. Paul, the tongue of Angels. Yet oftentimes they send forth an audible voice, as they that cried at the Ascension of Our Lord—"Ye men of Galilee, why stand ye here gazing into the heaven?" And in the old Law they speak to divers of the fathers with sensible voice; but this never but when they assumed bodies.

Agiel.	Belah.	Chemor.	Din.
45 ✱ 11	30 58	3 ✱ 11	5
Lætitia	Tristitia	Caput Draconis	Albus

Elim	Fabab	Graphiel.	Hecadoth
1 354 41	66 56 26	19 9	82 6
Fortuna minor	Fortuna major	Rubeus	Puella

Jah	Kne	Laked	Mehod
79 ✱ 13	2 8	120 64	6
Acquisitio	Cauda Draconis	Puer.	Amisio

Nebah.	Adonel	Pamiel.	Quedbarschemoch
Via.	Carcer.	Populus	Conjunctio.
Relah	Schethalim	Tiriel	Vabam
Carcer	Acquisitio	Letitia.	Puer.
Wasboga	Xoblah	Yschiel	Zelah
Amissio	Via	Populus	Conjunctio

Of Numbers, Their Power and Virtue

Boethius saith that all things from the beginning were formed from reason's numbers.

The Elements, change of times, motion of the stars and the heavens, and the state of all things, subsist by the joining together of Numbers. Time consists of number as also motion and action, and all things that are subject to time and motion. Concord in music and voices, have their power and proportion from Numbers and by lines and points constitute Characters and figures, and these are proper to Magical operations.

Themistrus and Averroes the Babylonian, with Plato do so extol Numbers, that they thought that no man could act the philosopher without them, but they meant Rational or Formal Number, not of the material, sensible or vocal, but they intended the proportion that resulted from that Number, which they call a Natural Number and a Formal and Rational, from which many holy things do flow from, as well in natural things as in divine and heavenly. By it we have an access to natural prophecy. A wonderful efficacious virtue lies hid in Numbers as well to good as evil.

Large volumes have been writ by Hebrew Doctors as Hieronymous, Augustine, Origen, Ambrose, Nazianzene, Athanasius, Basilius, Hillarius, Rabanus, Bede, and more others confirm this doctrine of the virtue of Numbers. And now in nature how great virtues Numbers possess is evident in the herb Cinquefoil.

The Number Seven works wonderful things—the seventh son to heal distempers. Whosoever shall know how to make vocal and natural numbers join with divine numbers and adequate their Constancy, may perform and know how to act wonderful things by these numbers.

The Pythagoreans foretold many events by the Numbers that attended Names, wherein lay hid a great mystery. St John in the Apocalypse speaks of the number of the Name which is the Number of a man, Lateinos 666.

Numbers operate much on the Soul, the figures on the bodies, but the harmony thereof on every animal.

Of Unity or the Number One

The powers and virtues of Numbers whereof Enoch's Tables are founded to be reckoned from Unity—Unitas omnem Numerum simplicissime penetriat, omniumque numerorum communis mensura, fons et origo.

There is one God, one world, one Sun of that world, one Phoenix in the world. One King among bees, one Captain in flocks. Among the members of the body, one is chief by which the rest is governed, whether it be the head or the heart. In the Elementary world, the Stone of the Philosophers which is the only subject and Instrument of all natural virtues and beyond the natural. In the Infernal world, Lucifer, the only prince of the rebellion of the Angels and darkness.

Of Duality or the Number Two

In the Archetype אֵל : יָהּ Nomina Dei duarum literarum.

In the Intellectual world, two substances Intelligible— the Angel, the Soul.

In the Heavenly world, two great Luminaries— the Sun, the Moon.

In the Elementary world, two Elements producing a living Soul— i.e. the earth, the Water.

In the Lesser World, two principal seats of the Soul— the Heart, the Brain.

In the Infernal world, two Captains of Demons— Behemoth, Leviathan...

Two things which Christ threatened to the damned—Weeping, Gnashing of Teeth.

Of the Triad or Number Three

The first number uncompounded and uneven, a holy Number perfect, most potent, for there are three persons in God, there are three Theological Virtues in religion — Faith, Hope and Charity.

The Name of God in 3 letters שַׁדָּי Sadai.

The whole measure of time in a Ternary— past, present and to come.

All magnitude contained in three things— a line, superfices, and a body.

Three kinds of Souls; a Vegetative, Sensitive and Intellectual— all three are in man.

In the lesser world— the head, the breast, the body— three parts answering the triple world.

In the Infernal world, three Infernal furies— Alecto, Megera, Tisiphone.

Three Infernal Judges— Minos, Aracus, Rhadamanthus.

Three degrees of the damned— Malefico, Apostates, Infidels.

Of the Number Four

Pythagoras preferred this Number as the root and foundation of all Numbers, from whence all foundations in artificial as well as divine things are quadrate, and signifies solidity.

The Name of God in four letters: יהוה

In the Intellectual world, unde Lex fatalis— four Triplicities or Hierarchies Intelligible.

Seraphim	Dominations	Principalities	Innocents
Cherubim	Powers	Archangels	Martyrs
Throni	Virtues	Angels	Confessors

Four Angel Presidents for governing the Cardinal points of Heaven

Michael	Raphael	Gabriel	Uriel

Quatuor praefecti Elementorum— four Governors of the Elements

Seraph	Cherub	Tharsis	Ariel
שרף	כרוב	תרשיש	אריאל

Four Sacred Animals

Leo	Aquila	Homo	Vitulus

Four Triplicities of the Tribes of Israel.

Dan	Jehuda	Manasse	Reuben
Asser	Isachar	Benjamin	Simeon
Nephthalim	Zabulon	Ephraim	Gad

Four Triplicities of the Apostles

Matthias	Symeon	John	Thaddeus
Petrus	Bartholomew	Phillip	Andreas
Jacobus Major	Matthew	Jacobus Minor	Thomas

Four Evangelists

Mark	John	Matthew	Luke

The four Triplicities of the Signs of the Zodiac

Aries	Gemini	Cancer	Taurus
Leo	Libra	Scorpio	Virgo
Sagittarius	Aquarius	Pisces	Capricornus

The Four Elements

The Stars and Planets as they are related to the Elements

Mars and	Jupiter and	Saturn and	Stella Fixae
Sol	Venus	Mercury	and Luna
Ignis	Aer	Aqua	Terra

The Four Qualities— Hot, Moist, Cold, Dry.

The Four Seasons— Summer, Spring, Winter, Autumn.

The Four Cardinal points of the World— East, West, North, South.

The Four Elements in Man— the Mind, the Spirit, the Soul, the Body.

The Four Powers of the Soul— the Intellect, the Reason, the Phantasy, the Senses.

The Four Moral Virtues— Justice, Temperance, Prudence, Fortitude.

The Four Elements of the Human body— the Spirit, the flesh, the humours, the bones.

The four Humours— Choler, Blood, Phlegme, Melancholy.

In the Infernal world, the four Princes of Demons that do hurt in the elements— Samael, Azazel, Azael, Mahazael.

The Four Infernal Rivers.

The four Princes of Demons governing the four Quarters of the World— Oriens, Paymon, Aegyn, Amaymon.

Of the Number Five

This number hath a great force in Expiations. For in holy things it drives away bad Demons, in natural things it expells poisons. Also it is called a Number of felicity and grace, and is the seal of the spirit of grace, the number of Christ's wounds on the Cross.

The names of God of five letters,

אליון Elion   אלהים Elohim   יהשוה Ihesuh

In the Intellectual world there are five Intelligible substances—

1. The Spirits of the first Hierarchy called Gods, or the Sons of God,

2. The Spirits of the second Hierarchy called Intelligences,

3. The Spirits of the third Hierarchy called Angels which are sent,

4. The Souls of heavenly bodies,

5. Heroes or Blessed Souls.

In the Celestial world, five wandering stars, Lords of the Terms— Saturn, Jupiter, Mars, Venus, Mercury.

In the Elemental world— Water, Air, Fire, Earth, a mixture of the Elements.

The five species of mixed beings— Living Creatures, Plant, Metal, a Stone, Zoophylum, or that are in part living creatures in part plants, as sponges, oysters.

In the Lesser world, the five senses— Tasting, Hearing, Seeing, Touching, Smelling.

In the Infernal World, the five corporeal torments— Bitterness mortifying, horrible haulings, terrible darkness, burning that cannot be quenched, stink that penetrateth.

Of the Number Six

In the whole context of Numbers, six is the most perfect Number in Nature. It is so perfect, that by the collection of its parts, the same results; for if the parts, to with, the middle, the third and the sixth, which are three, two and one, are gathered together, they do perfectly fill up the body of six, which perfection other numbers want. The sixth day the world was made, and the heavens and Earth and the adornments thereof.

It is called the number of a man, because on the sixth day Man was created. In the Law it was ordained, six days to work, six days to gather Manna, six years to sow the Earth, a Hebrew servant to serve six years his master, six days the glory of God inclined upon Mount Sinai covering it with a cloud. A Cherub had six wings. There were six circles in the firmament—the Arctic, the Antarctic, two Tropics, the Aequinoctial and Ecliptic; six planets that err— Saturn, Jupiter, Mars, Venus, Mercurius, Luna—running through the latitude of the Zodiac, running on this and the other side of the Ecliptic. A solid quadrate figure hath six superfices. There are six tones of all Harmony, viz., 5 tones and two semitones which make up one tone, which is a sixth.

In the Elementary world, there are six substantific qualities of the Elements— Rest, Thinness, Sharpness, Bluntness, Density, Motion.

In the lesser world, six degrees of Man— Intellectus, Memoria, Sensus, Motus, Vita, Essentia.

In the Infernal world, six Demons, the authors of all calamities— Acteus, Megalesius, Ormenius, Lycus, Nicon, Mimo.

The Name of God of six letters אלגבור אֲלוֹהִים

Of the Number Seven

The Number Seven is of a divers and manifold power. It consists of one and six, or of two and five, or of three and four, and it hath an unity as a Copula or joining together a double trinity. It is a Number full of all Majesty. The Pythagoreans call it the vehicle of human life, for this Number comprehends soul and body, for the body consists of the four Elements and is affected with four qualities; the ternary also belongs to the Soul, by reason of his triple force, that is, his rational, irascible and corruptible. Therefore, the septenary Number, which consists of three and four joins the soul to the body, and the force of this number seven pertains to the geniture of man. Plato in his *Timaeus*, hath writ largely concerning this Number seven, as to its power and wonderful operation in the generation, geniture of man and vicissitudes every seventh year. Pythagoras called Seven a Number of virginity, because it is the first which is neither generated not doth generate, neither can it be divided into two equal parts, so as it may be produced of any repeated number, neither of itself brings forth any number of a duplicate, which may be brought within the limits of ten, which is the first limit of numbers, and therefore the seventh Number was sacred to Pallas. In religion this number is venerated, it is called the Number of an oath among the Hebrews, so Abraham when he made a League with Abimilech he appointed seven ewe lambs in testimony. And it is called the Number of blessedness and rest. The seventh day, the Creator rested from his works, therefore this day with Moses is called the Sabbath, that is a day of rest. Through the Old and New Testaments we find many times Seven recorded, and many mysteries in the Apocalypse comprehending the number Seven. The Number Seven hath many powers as well in natural things as in holy thing and ceremonies—seven days, seven planets, seven pleiades, seven ages of the world, seven changes of man, seven liberal arts as many mechanical, seven colours, seven metals.

In the Archetypal world, the Name of God in seven letters,

אראריתא	Ararita
אשר אהיה	Asser Eheie

In the Intelligible world, seven Angels which stand before the face of God— Zaphkiel, Zadkiel, Camael, Raphael, Haniel, Michael. These are Hebrew names of God as to his Attributes which names the seven Angels that govern this sublunary world do bear.

In the Celestial world, the seven planets— Saturnus, Jupiter, Mars, Sol, Venus, Mercury, Luna.

In the Elemental world

♄	♃	♂	☉	♀	☿	☽

seven Birds—

♄	♃	♂	☉	♀	☿	☽
Upupa	Aquilo	Vultur	Olor	Columba	Ciconia	Noctua
Lapwing	Eagle	Vulture	Swan	Dove	Stork	Owl

seven Fishes—

♄	♃	♂	☉	♀	☿	☽
Sepia	Delphinus	Lucius	Vitulus	Thimallus	Mugil	Aelurus
Cuttle	Dolphin	Pike	Sea Cow		Mullet	Seal

seven Animals—

♄	♃	♂	☉	♀	☿	☽
Talpa	Cervus	Lupus	Leo	Hircus	Simia	Feles
Moles	Deer	Wolf	Lion	Goat	Ape	Cat

seven Metals—

♄	♃	♂	☉	♀	☿	☽
Plumbum	Stannum	Ferrum	Aurum	Cuprum	Argentum Vive	Argentum
Lead	Tin	Iron	Gold	Copper	Quicksilver	Silver

seven Stones—

♄	♃	♂	☉	♀	☿	☽
Onychmus	Sapphirus	Adamas	Carbunculus	Achates		Chrystallus ?
Onyx	Sapphire	Diamond	Carbuncle			Crystal

In the Infernal world, seven habitations of the damned, which Rabbi Joseph Castiliensis describes in *Hocto nucis*—

גיהנם	Gehenna	בארשהת	Puteus Inferitus
וצלמות	Portae Mortis	טיטהיון	Lutum fecis
ידעשתום	Umbra Mortis	אכרוז	Perditio
		שאול	Fovea

Of the Number Eight

The Pythagoreans call it a Number of Justice and plenitude, because first of all it is divided into numbers alike even, that is to say into four, and that division is made twice two, and for the equality of its division it assumes the name of Justice. And for its other name of plenitude, because it makes a solid body. Hence, Orpheus swearing by eight Deities to implore divine Justice, viz., fire, water, earth, heaven, Moon, Sun, Phanes, and the night.

There are also only eight visible spheres of the heavens, and the propriety of corporeal nature is signified to us by him which Orpheus comprehended in his Octonary of maritime hymns. And this number is also called a number of league and Circumcision which by the Jews was instituted to be done on the eighth day.

This number pertains to Eternity, and the end of the worlds, because it follows the seventh number, which is the symbol of time. Hence this number is of beautitude, for so many degrees of blessedness, Christ taught in Matthew. It is also called a number of safety and conservation, for so many souls were saved in Noah from the deluge of waters.

This number was esteemed holy by Dionysius, who came into the world in the eighth month, unto the everlasting memory of him the Island Naxos was dedicated to him, and obtained this prerogative that only the women of Naxia brought forth healthful children in the eighth month, when almost all those born so in other nations died and their mothers also lay under manifest danger.

The Names of God in Eight letters:

| אלוה ודעת | Eloha Vedaath |
| יהוה ודעת | Tetragrammaton Vedaath |

In the Intelligible world, the eight rewards of the blessed— an Inheritance, Incorruption, Power, Victory, Vision of God, Grace, a Kingdom, Joy.

In the Celestial world— the Starry heaven, the heaven of Saturn, the heaven of Jupiter, the heaven of Mars, the heaven of the Sun, the heaven of Venus, the heaven of Mercury, the heaven of the Moon.

In the Elemental World, eight particular qualities— the dryness of the earth, the coldness of the water, the humidity of the air, the heat of the fire, the heat of the air, the humidity of the water, the dryness of the fire, the coldness of the earth.

In the Lesser world, eight sorts of blessed men— the peaceable, those that hunger and thirst after righteousness, the meek, persecuted for righteousness, pure in heart, merciful, poor in spirit, mourning.

In the Infernal world, eight rewards of the damned— a Prison, Death, Judgment, Anger of God, Indignation, Tribulation, Anguish, (?).

Of the Number Nine

This number was sacred to the Muses; there are nine Moveable Spheres, and nine Muses, everyone relating to the spheres—Calliope is accommodated to the primum mobile, Urania to the starry heaven, Polyhymnia to Saturn, Terpsichore to Jupiter, Clio to Mars, Melpomene to the Sun, Erato to Venus, Euterpe to Mercury, Thalia to the Moon.

There are Nine Orders of Blessed Angels, that is to say— Seraphim, Cherubim, Thrones, Dominations, Virtues, Powers, Principalities, Archangels, Angels, which Ezechiel figures out by nine Stones, which are these— the Sapphire, Smarag, Carbuncle, Beryl, Onyx, Chrysolite, Jasper, Topaz, Sardius.

This Number is of a sacramental great and occult quality, at the ninth hour Jesus expired, and in nine days the Ancients buried their dead, and in so many years Minea in a den received the Laws from Jove, from hence this number was chiefly observed by Homer, and Astrologers of old had the same esteem for Novenary years as well as Septenary, which was equally reckoned Climacterical, wherein they observed notable mutations. But sometimes this Number hath a note of imperfection and defect, because it reaches not to the perfection of a Denary, but is less than an unity, as in the Gospel, of the 10 lepers, but where are the nine. Neither doth it want a mystery, the longitude of Og, King of Basan, who was nine cubits long, but he was a type of the devil.

The Names of God in Nine letters

יהוה צאבאות	Tetragrammaton Sabaoth
יהוה צדקנו	Tetragrammaton Zidkenu
אלהים גיבר	Elohim Gibor

In the Intelligible world, the nine Choirs of Angels— Seraphim, Cherubim, Thrones, Dominations, Powers, Virtues, Principalities,

Archangels, Angels. The nine Angel presidents in the heavens—
Metratton, Ophaniel, Zaphkiel, Zadkiel, Camael, Raphael, Haniel,
Michael, Gabriel.

In the Celestial world— Primum Mobile, Caelum Stellarum,
Sphera Saturni, Sphera Jovis, Sphera Martis, Sphera Solis, Sphera
Veneris, Sphera Mercurii, Sphera Lunae.

The nine Stones— Sapphirus, Smaragdus, Carbunculus, Beril-
lus, Onyx, Chrysolithus, Jaspis, Topazius, Sardius.

In the Lesser world, the nine senses as well outward as in-
ward— Memory, Cogitation, Imagination, Common Sense, Hearing, Seeing, Smelling, Tasting, Touching.

In the Infernal world, nine Orders of Cacodemons— Pseudothei, Spiritus medarii, Vasa Iniquitatis, Ultores Scelerum, Praestigiatores, Aereae potestates, Furiae seminatrices malorum,
Criminatores sive exploratores, Tentatores sive Infidiatores.

Of the Decade or Ten

Ten, this every number is called, whether an Universal or a
number complete, denoting the full course of life, for from this
number beyond it we cannot number except by replication, and it
implies all numbers either within itself, or by itself it resolves them
by multiplication, whereof it is esteemed of a manifold religion and
power, and fitted for the purging of our hearts. Hence the Ancients
abstained from certain things ten days using denary ceremonies for
expiation; thence it was a custom with the Egyptians that whosoever was initiated in the sacred rites of Isis, were wont to fast ten
days, which Apuleius testified of himself.

This Number as a Unity is also circular, because being heaped
together it returns into an Unity from whence it had beginning, for
it is the end and complement of all Numbers and the beginning of
Decades.As a denary flows back into Unity from whence it proceeded, so the water runs to the sea from whence it had its original.

The Name of God in Ten Letters:

אלהים צבאות Elohim Sabaoth

In the Intelligible world, the ten orders of blessed spirits according to the Hebrews— Haioth Hakados, Ophani, Aralim, Hasmalim, Seraphim, Malachim, Elohim, Ben Elohim, Cherubim, Issim.

Ten Angel Presidents— Mettratton, Iophiel, Zaphkiel, Zadkiel, Camael, Raphael, Haniel, Michael, Gabriel, Anima Messiah.

Ten Mundane spheres— Primum Mobile, Sphera Zodiaci, Sphera Saturni, Sphera Jovis, Sphera Martis, Sphera Solis, Sphera Veneris, Sphera Mercurii, Sphera Lunae, Sphera Elementorum.

In the Elemental world, ten sacred animals relating to the heathen Gods— Columba, Pardus, Draco, Aquilo, Equus, Leo, Homo, Serpens, Bos, Agnus.

In the Infernal world, the ten Orders of the Damned— Pseudothei, Spiritus medarii, Vasa Iniquitatis, Ultores Scelerna, Praestigiatores, Aeriae potestates, Furiae seminatrices malorum, Criminatores sive exploratores, Tentatores sive Justitiatores, Anima provae et Damnata.

Of the Number Eleven
The Eleventh Number as it exceeds the tenth, which is the number of the Law and Commandments. Therefore it is called the number of sinners and penitents, hence this number hath no communion with divine things, nor heavenly, nor ladder tending to heaven, nor any merit, but sometimes perchance receives a grateful favour from God, as he who at the eleventh hour was called into God's vineyard, he received the reward of them who bore the burden and heat of the day.

Of the Number Twelve
The Twelfth Number is divine, wherein heavenly things are measured. Twelve signs in the Zodiac, wherein twelve chief Angels preside bearing names of the great God. In twelve years Jupiter performs his course around the heavens, and the Moon daily runs through twelve degrees.

The Names of God in twelve letters:

הקרש	והוה	כאבו
Pater	Filius	Spiritus Sanctus

In the Intelligible world, the twelve Orders of blessed Spirits—Seraphim, Cherubim, Throni, Dominations, Potestates, Virtues, Principalities, Archangels, Angels, Innocents, Martyrs, Confessors.

The twelve Angels president over the signs— Malachael, Asmodel, Ambriel, Muriel, Nerchiel, Hamaliel, Zwael, Barbiel, Adachiel, Hanael, Gabriel, Barchiel.

The twelve tribes — the twelve Prophets — the twelve Apostles — in the Celestial world, the twelve signs of the Zodiac — the twelve months — twelve plants in the Elemental world — twelve stones in Aaron's Breastplate — twelve principal members of man, head, neck, arms, etc., in the lesser world.

In the Infernal world, twelve degrees of Damned Spirits and Devils— Pseudothei, Spiritus medarii, Vasa Iniquitatis, Ultores Scelerum, Praestigiatores, Aeriae potestates, Furiae seminatrices malorum, Criminatores seu exploratores, Tentatores seu Justitiatores, Malefici, Apostatae, Infideles.

Of Other Numbers, their Power and Virtue

13   The Thirteenth day after Christ's birth, a star guided the Magi to Christ.

14   The Fourteenth is a type of (relating to Christ, who was offered the fourteenth day of the first month — the going out of Egypt.

15   The Fifteenth, a spiritual number of Ascensions, and therefore a song of degrees on fifteen Psalms was made. Fifteen years was added to Ezechia's reign.

16   The Sixteenth is a Number of an equilateral square body, called by Pythagoras a Number of felicity. For it comprehends all the prophets of the Old Testament as well as all the Apostles and Evangelists of the New Testament.

18   These Numbers by Divines are reckoned unfortunate.

20   Israel served Eglon King of Moab 18 years, Jacob served, Joseph was sold.

22   The Number 22 signifies the fulness of wisdom, so many are the Hebrew letters, and so many books the Old Testament contains.

28   The Number 28 attributed to the Moon who completes her course through the Zodiac in twenty eight days.

30   The Number 30 is full of Mysteries, the price put on our Saviour, at 30 years he was baptised. John the Baptist preached at 30. Ezechiel prophesied at 30.

32   A number of Wisdom as the Hebrew Doctors assert, for so many paths of wisdom are described of Abraham. The Pythagoreans style this number of Justice which may be divided into equal parts even to Unity.

40   The Ancients worship this Number with great veneration, from whence they celebrated the Feast of Tesseracoston. This number is full of mysteries, a number for Expiation and penitence in religion. 40 days the Deluge. 40 years the Children of Israel lived in the Desert. 40 days before the Subversion of Nineveh. 40 days Moses, Elias, and Christ fasted. 40 weeks Christ was borne in the womb of the Virgin. 40 days from the Nativity, Christ was in Bethlehem before he was offered in the Temple. 40 months he preached publicly. 40 hours he lay in the sepulchre. The 40th day after his resurrection he ascended into heaven.

50   The 50th number is significative for remission of sins, and servitude and liberty. According to the law, debts were remitted in the 50th year, and every one was returned into their own possession—a year of Jubilee. On the 50th day of the Israelites going out of Egypt the law was given. The 50 day after the resurrection, the Holy Ghost descended upon the Apostles in Mount Zion. From hence it is called a number of grace, and attributed to the Holy Ghost.

60   A number sacred to the Egyptians and proper to the Crocodile, who for 60 days brings forth eggs, and in so many days nourishes them, is said to live 40 years, and hath 40 teeth, and lastly every year for 40 days sequesters himself from meat.

70   This number contains great Mysteries. 70 years the face of

the sacrifice did live lying hid under water during the Babylonian captivity. So many years Jeremiah foretold the destruction of the Temple. So many years lasted the Captivity of Babylon. So many years completed the desolation of Jerusalem. Cum multis aliis.

72   This many languages are recorded. So many Elders of the Synagogue. So many Interpreters of the Bible. So many Disciples of Christ. It hath great communion with the Number Twelve. Hence in Celestials every sign divided into 6 parts, there result 72 Quinaries, over which are president so many Angels, and so many Names of God bear influence, and every quinary is set over one Idiom with so great efficacy, that thence Astrologers and Physiognomers can know of what idiom or planet any one was born under. So many patent arteries in the human body answer them, of which in every finger of hand and foot are reckoned three, which with the principal twelve above in the 12 accounted, do constitute 72.

100 Centenary, in which a sheep found is collocated who also passes from the left to the right, is found sacred, as also from ten generated designs a complete perfection.

1000 But the complement of all numbers is the Millenary, which is the Cube of ten, signifying consummate and absolute perfection.

There are two numbers celebrated very much by Plato and Aristotle in his *Politics*, which have proved ominous to Kingdoms and portended great mutations in cities. These numbers are the Square of 12 and his Cube, to wit, the 44th above a hundred, and 728th above a thousand which number is fatal.

Of the Numbers that the Ancients Consecrated to Their Gods and Ascribed to the Elements and Planets

The Pythagoreans dedicated certain Numbers sacred to the Elements and heavenly bodies. To the Air and Octonary, to the Fire a Tetragon, to the Earth a Senary, to the Water a Duodenary number they assigned. Moreover, they ascribed unity to the Sun, because he is the only King of the stars, wherein God placed his Tabernacle. They ascribed the same to Jupiter, who was the father and head of the Gods, as unity is the beginning and parent of Numbers.

Duality is given to the Moon, which is the second luminary, and figures out the Soul of the World, and is called Juno, because between her and unity there is the first conjunction and alike concord. It is also given to Saturn and Mars, the two Infortunes with Astrologers.

The Number Three agrees with Jupiter, the Sun and Venus, the three fortunes, it is also deputed to Vesta, Hecate and Diana. This triad is therefore dedicated to this virgin, which they say is powerful both in heaven and hell.

Four or the Quaternary Number belongs to the Sun who by that number constitutes the cardinal points of heaven and the seasons or times of the year, it is also deputed to Cillenius which was the only quadrate God esteemed.

Five or a Quinary is assigned to Mercury from one parity and one imparity, as it is manifest from either sex, masculine or feminine. Also it is attributed to the heavenly world, which above the four elements is the fifth under another form.

A Senary pertains to Venus and Jupiter, which is made up of a triad led by a dyad, which number Pythagoras is accommodated to generation and marriage.

Septenary, a number of rest, belongs to Saturn. The same number concerns the Moon's motion and light. It is assigned to Minerva who hath no generation, also to Pallas that virago, because it consists of numbers as well masculine as feminine. Plutarch gives this number to Apollo.

The Eighth number belongs to Jupiter, sacred to Justice and it is dedicated to Vulcan. It is attributed to Cybele, the Mother of the Gods, to whom every Cube is given. Plutarch assigned that number to Bacchus or Dionysius, who was born in the eighth month; because others born in the eighth month died, they constituted that number to Saturn and the Parcae.

The number Nine belongs to the Moon, the last receptacle of all celestial influences and virtues, no less than if it were dedicated to the nine muses, as also to Mars from whom is the end of all things.

The tenth number is circular because Monas or Unity belongs to the Sun. Also it is assigned to Juno. In like manner the Twelfth number, because the Sun goes through the 12 signs in 12 months. This number is given to the world, to the heaven, and to the Sun. But the eleventh number because it is semicircular is attributed to the Moon and deputed also to Neptune.

Of the Little Tables of the Planets
and what Divine Names, Intelligences and Demons Belong to these Tables

The Magi of old framed certain Tables distributed to the seven planets. They called them sacred containing great virtues of heavenly things because they represent the divine reason of heavenly numbers, by the Ideas of a divine soul, by a reason impressed on the Soul of the World in heavenly things, and the sweet harmony of those heavenly things, according to the proportion of the effigies, signifying together the Intelligences more than mundane, which cannot otherwise be expressed than by the notes of numbers and characters. For material numbers and figures can do nothing in the mysteries of hidden things unless represented by numbers and formal figures as they are governed and informed by the Intelligences and Divine numerations, which unite the extremes of matter and spirit, to the will of the soul elevated by a great affection of the operator in celestial virtue, receiving power from God, by the Soul of the Universe, and the observations of celestial constellations, unto a matter applied to a form convenient, by disposed mediums in the skill and science magical.

Saturn's Table consists of a quadrate ternary containing nine particular numbers. In every line three numbers which make 15. To this Table are prefixed Names filling up these numbers, with an Intelligence for good, and a Demon for evil. From the same Numbers are found the seal and character of Saturn and his spirits.

This Table engraved on a plate of Lead and worn about you, Saturn being fortunate, helps childbirth, makes a man safe and powerful in his petitions to great persons, but if Saturn be unfortunate, it casts a man down from honours and dignities, increases strife and discord.

Tabula Saturni in Notis Hebraicis.

ד 4	ט 9	ב 2
ג 3	ה 5	ז 7
ח 8	א 1	ו 6

Divine names answering to the Number of Saturn.

Ab . 3 .   אב :

Hod . 9 .   חד :

Jah . 15 .   יה :

Agiel 45 .   אגיאל :

Zazel . 45 .   אזאל :

_____

אָגִיאָל׃   ·   אז ז ל :

Signacula sive Characteres Saturni

Intelligentia Saturni .   *Dæmon Saturni*

Jupiter's Table consists of a quaternary in itself containing 16 particular numbers. The total sum is 136. And there are set over it the Divine names with an Intelligence to good, and a Demon for evil, and the character of Jove and of his spirits is allured by it.

If this table be engraven on a silver plate, Jupiter potent and ruling, gain and riches will attend him that wears it, favour and love, peace and concord. It will dissolve witchcraft being engraven in Coral.

The Table of Jupiter

ד 4	יד 14	טו 15	א 1
ט 9	ז 7	ו 6	יב 12
ה 5	יא 11	י 10	ח 8
יו 16	ב 2	ג 3	יג 13

Divine Names answering
the Numbers of Jupiter.

Abba . 4   אבא :

El Ab. 34   אל אב :

Jophiel. 136 : יהפיאל
Intelligentia Jovis.

Hismael 136 : הסמאל
Damonium Jovis

Intelligences of Jupiter

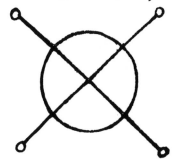

Damonij Jovis

The Table of Mars hath a quinary square containing in the whole numbers 25. In every line, side and diameter, 65. The total sum is 325. Over which presides Divine names with Intelligences to good and a Demon to do evil, and from hence is allured the Character of Mars and of his spirits.

This table engraven on an Iron Lamen or Sword, makes him that bears it valiant in war and terrible to his adversaries, and shall conquer his enemies. And if it be cut in Cornelian stone it stops bleeding and the menstrua. But if Mars proves unfortunate let it be graven on a Lamen of red brass. It casts down the potent from dignities and honours and riches, breeds discord and contentions and hatred of man and beast, makes unfortunate those that go a hunting and to the wars, causeth sterility or barrenness in men, women and other creatures.

Tabula Martis in Notis Hebraicis.

יא 11	כד 24	ז 7	ב 20	ג 3
ר 4	יב 12	בה 25	ה 8	יו 16
יז 17	ה 5	יג 13	בא 21	ט 9
י 10	יח 18	א 1	יר 14	בב 22
גב 23	י 6	יט 19	ב 2	יה 15

Divino Names Answering the Numbers of Mars.

Ho ~ 5 : ה

Adonai ~ 65 : אדני

$\overline{325}$
Graphiel : גראפיאל

Intelligentia Martis.

325 : ברצאבאל

Barzabel. Dæmonium Martis.

Intelligentia Martis   Dæmonij Martis

The Table of the Sun consists of a Senary quadrate. It contains numbers 36; whereof 6 in every side and diameter produce 111, and the sum of all is 666. The Divine names preside with an Intelligence to good and a Demon for mischief, and from thence are alluded the Characters of the Sun and his spirits.

This Table graved on a golden Lamen, the Sun being fortunate, makes the bearer glorious, lovely, beloved, grateful, powerful in all works and makes a man a companion for Kings and Princes, elevating a man to the top of fortune's wheel to command what he will. But the Sun unfortunate makes him a tyrant, proud and ambitious and to make an ill end.

The Table of the Sun in Hebrew notes.

ו	לב	ג	לד	לה	א
6	12	3	34	35	1
ז	יא	בז	בח	ה	ל
7	11	27	28	8	30
יט	יד	יו	יה	כג	כד
19	14	16	15	23	24
יה	יב	בב	כא	יז	יג
18	20	22	21	17	13
בה	בט	י	ט	בו	יב
25	29	10	9	26	12
לו	ה	גל	ד	ב	לא
36	5	33	4	2	31

Divine names answering the Numbers of ▮▮▮ The Sun

: ו, *vau*, a Letter of the holy name. 6

: הא *He*, a letter of the holy name 6:

: אלה *Eloh.* ———————— 36

: נכיאל *Nachiel. Intelligence of the Sun.* 111

: סורת *Sorath. Dæmonium Solis* 666.

The Table of Venus consists of a Septenary in numbers 49; whereof 7 in every side and Diameter constitute 175, and the sum of them all amount to 1225. And they bear the names of God with an Intelligence to good and a Demon to evil, and from thence the Character of Venus and her Spirits is drawn.

This Table engraved on a Lamen of Silver, Venus being Fortunate, reconciles and makes concord, takes away contentions, gives the love of women. Further it helps conception, takes away barrenness, makes powerful to generation, dissolves witchcraft, generates peace between man and wife and all other creatures, makes flocks of cattle fruitful, and being put in a dovecot, multiplies pigeons. A sovereign remedy against all griefs that proceed from melancholy, creates joy and makes fortunate travellers that wear it. But if it be formed in brass, Venus unfortunate, then understand the contrary.

The Table of Venus in Hebrew Notes.

בב 22	מז 47	יו 16	מא 41	י 10	לה 15	ד 4
ה 5	כג 23	מר 48	יז 17	מכ 42	יא 11	בט 29
ל 30	ו 6	בד 24	מש 49	יח 18	לו 36	יב 12
יג 13	לא 31	ו 7	כה 25	מג 43	יט 19	לז 37
לה 38	יד 14	לב 32	א 1	כו 26	מד 44	ב 20
בא 21	לט 39	ח 8	לג 33	ב 2	כז 27	מה 45
מו 46	יח 15	מ 40	ט 9	לר 34	ג 3	בח 28

הניאל — 49
Hagiel an Intelligence of Venus

אתא — 7

קדמאל 157
Kademel
Dæmonium
Veneris.

בני שרפים: Ben Seraphim Intelligentia Veneris

Signacula seu Characteres Veneris

Intelligentia Veneris
Intelligentiarū Veneris

Dæmonij Veneris.

The Table of Mercury results from an Octonary containing numbers 64, whereof 8 in every side and by either diameter do make 260, and the sum of all is 2080. And to it is affixed the Divine names with Intelligence to good and a Demon to mischief and from thence is brought the Character of Mercury and his spirits.

And if it shall be engraven, Mercury being fortunate, in Silver, Tin or Brass, or written in Virgin parchment it will make him that wears it fortunate to obtain whatsoever he desires, it confers gain and expells want, it gives a memory and understanding, and divination and knowledge of occult things by dreams. And if Mercury prove unfortunate then judge the contrary.

The Table of Mercury in Hebrew Note

רח 8	חמ 58	מש 59	ה 5	רד 4	סב 62	סג 63	א 1
מט 49	יה 15	יר 14	נב 52	נג 53	יא 11	י 10	נו 56
מא 41	כג 23	כב 22	מר 44	מה 45	יט 19	יח 18	מח 48
לב 32	לר 34	לה 35	כט 29	כח 28	לח 38	לט 39	כה 25
מ 40	כו 26	כז 27	לז 37	לו 36	ל 30	לא 31	לג 33
יז 17	מז 47	מו 46	כ 20	כא 21	מג 43	מב 42	כד 24
ט 9	נה 55	נר 54	יב 12	יג 13	נא 51	נ 50	יו 16
סר 64	ב 2	ג 3	סא 61	ס 60	י 6	ז 7	נז 57

Signacula sive Characteres

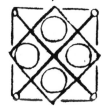

Mercurij

Intelligentia Mercurij

Dæmonij Mercurij

The Table of the Moon consists of a Novenary in itself multiplied in itself, having numbers 81; in every side and diameter 9, producing 369, and the sum of all is 3321 and there preside over it the Divine names with Intelligences to good and a Demon to evil. And there is drawn out from it Characters of the Moon and of his spirits.

This Table engraven in silver, the Moon fortunate, makes the bearer thereof, lovely, grateful, pleasant, cheerful, honoured, taking away all malice and ill will; makes one secure in traveling and getting riches, sound in body. It expells enemies and other hurtful things from any place that you desire. And if this table be made on a Lamen of Lead, wheresoever you shall bury it, that place shall be unfortunate, and the inhabitants therein, as also ships, fountains, rivers, mills. It will make unfortunate every man against whom it shall be rightly made, making him a profligate or vagabond in his country and mansion place where it shall lie buried.

The Table of the Moon ☽ in Hebrew notes

לי	עה	כט	ע	בא	סב	גי	מה	ה
37	78	29	70	21	62	13	45	5
ו	לה	עט	ל	עא	כב	סג	יד	מו
6	38	79	30	71	22	63	14	46
מז	ז	לט	פ	לא	עכ	כג	נח	יה
47	7	39	80	31	72	23	55	15
יו	מה	ה	מ	פא	לב	סר	כד	נו
16	48	8	40	81	32	64	24	56
נז	יז	מט	ט	מא	עג	לג	סה	בח
57	17	49	9	41	73	33	65	25
כו	נה	יה	נ	א	מב	עד	לד	סו
26	58	18	50	1	42	74	34	66
סז	בז	נט	י	נא	ב	מג	עה	לה
67	27	59	10	51	2	43	75	35
לו	סח	יט	ס	יא	נב	ג	מר	עי
36	68	19	60	11	52	3	44	76
שז	נח	סט	ב	כא	יכ	נג	ד	מה
77	28	69	20	61	12	53	4	45

Signacula sive Characteres

Lune -

Damonij Lune

Damonij Damoni-orum Lune

Intelligentia - Intelligentiarum Lune -

Gevah Shehakim 3321.

Of the Sun and Moon
Magically Understood and Explained

The Platonists esteemed the Sun to be the Soul of the World, the Lord of all Elemental virtues, and the Moon by the virtue of the Sun is the Lady of Generation, of increase and decrease. The Sun and Moon are the lively eyes of Heaven infusing life to all things. The Sun plentifully gives light from itself to all things, not only in the heaven and air, but also in the earth and profound Abyss. Whatsoever good we have proceeds from the Sun, the Sun being the fountain of heavenly light, the heart of heaven and placed in the middle of the planets, the most exact Image of God whose Essence is of the nature of the Father, Splendour the Son, Heat the Holy Ghost. The Sun is the conspicuous Son of God, the Image of Divine Intelligence. So many motions there are in the mind, as every day the Sun may bring, who is the prince and the moderator of the planets.

But the Moon, being nearest the Earth of all the planets, is the receptacle of all Coelestial Influxes, joining issue monthly with the Sun and the rest of the planets and stars, the supposed wife of all the stars, bringing the rays and influences of all the planets and stars to this lower world.

The motion of the Moon is chiefly to be observed before all other planets, she is the parent of all conceptions. Consider her complexion, motion, site and aspects which differ from the planets and the other stars, and although she may get strength from all the stars, chiefly from the Sun so often as she is joined to him, she is filled with a lively virtue and as she beholds them alters complexion, for in the first quarter she is hot and moist, in the second hot and dry, in the third cold and dry, in the fourth cold and moist.

From the Moon in heavenly matters begins the series of things which Plato called the Golden Chain. Observe the Rule that if you will take the virtue of any star, you must take a stone and herb of the nature of that star which from the Moon happily beholds that star.

Of the Soul of the World, Proved

That the Soul of the World and Heavenly Souls are rational and do partake of a divine mind.

The Soul of the World is defined to be vita quodam unica, a certain only life, filling all things, pouring forth all things from every part, gathering together and connecting all things, that it may become one machine of the whole world; and that it may be as one Monochord, sounding, again from the three kinds of Creatures only by one breath and one life, Intellectual, Celestial and Incorruptible.

That human Imprecations do naturally impress their strength upon outward things. And that how the human mind ascends into the intelligible world by every degree of dependencies and is made like to the spirits and more sublime Intelligences.

Of Intelligences and Daemons
Three Sorts of Them, Their Divers Names
And of Infernal and Subterranean Daemons

An Intelligence is a substance intelligible, free from all gross putrefying mass of body, Immortal, insensible, influencing all things. And there is the same nature of all Intelligences, spirits and Daemons. But those Daemons are not those which we call Devils, but spirits so called from the propriety of the word, as knowing, intelligent and wise. But of those Daemons there are three kinds according to the tradition of the Magi, whereof they call the first Supercoelestial, and minds in a manner disjoined from the body, and in a manner intellectual spheres, worshipping one God as their most firm established unity or Centre, whereof they call them Gods, by a certain participation of divinity, because always they are full with God, and drunk with Divine Nectar. They are only conversant about one God, neither are they set over the bodies of the world, nor adapted to the ministration of Inferior things, but influence the light they have from God to inferior Orders.

Next to these in a second Order follow the Heavenly Intelligences which they call Mundane Daemons, to wit accommodated to the spheres beyond the divine worship of the world, these Intelligences are president of the stars in every heaven. Hence they distribute them into so many orders as there are heavens in the world and stars in the heavens, and they called others Saturnians, who were set over the heaven of Saturn, and Saturn himself: others were Jovians who presided or were set over the heaven of Jupiter or Jupiter himself. In like manner, they gave names to other Daemons by the name and virtue of other stars: and because the ancient Astrologers did assert 55 motions, hence to these they found out as many Intelligences or Daemons. And they placed in the starry heaven, Daemons who they set over the Signs and Triplicities, Decans and Quinaries, degrees and stars. They placed twelve chief Daemons, who were set over the Twelve Signs of the Zodiac, and 36 who were set over so many Decans or faces of the Signs, every Sign containing three faces, and 72 besides were set over so many

Quinaries of heaven, so many Linguas and Nations of heaven. And 4 they set over the Triplicities and Elements: and 7 Governors of the whole world according to the seven planets, and they gave names to all these and Seals, which they call Characters, and used them in Invocations and Incantations and their Sculptures, describing them in Instruments of their own operations, in Images, Lamens, glasses, rings, paper and the like made of wax, that when they made an operation to the Sun, they Invocated by the names of the Sun, and by the names of the Solar Daemons, and so of the rest.

Thirdly, they put Daemons as Ministers to dispose of things Earthly in inferior things, which Origen calls certain invisible virtues which none can behold, which direct our journeys and business. They are oft set over battles, and give wishes for success to our friends and secret relief, to reconcile in prosperity and inflict in adversary, as you please.

In like manner they distribute them into more orders these distinctions of Daemons according to the Elements are fiery, watery, aerial, and earthly, which four spheres of Daemons are compelled according to the strength of the four coelestial souls. For aerial Daemons follow the reason and favour the rational power, separating it after a sort from sensual and vegetable. Therefore, they serve the active life, as the fiery serve the contemplative life. But the watery Daemons follow the Imagination and sense, they serve the voluptuous life. Earthy Daemons follow nature, they favour vegetal nature. Furthermore they distinguish this kind of Daemon into Saturnians and Jovials according to the names of the stars and of the heavens. Besides, some Daemons are Oriental, others Occidental, others Meridional, others Septentrional. Lastly, no part of the world is destitute without the assistance of these Daemons: not because they are there only, but because they most reign there: for they are everywhere, although some most strongly operate, and have influence elsewhere. Neither are these things so to be understood as if they were subject to the influxes of the stars, but that they may answer to the supra-mundane heaven, from which chiefly all things are directed and to which all things ought to be Conformable, hence as these Demons are adapted to divers places and seasons, not that they are restrained to time or place, but because the order of wisdom hath so decreed it; therefore they more favour and defend those bodies, places, times, stars; so they called these Daemons some diurnal, some nocturnal, some meridian. In like manner, they call some Daemons of the woods, others mountains, others of the valleys, others domestic. Hence the Sylvans, Satyrs, Nymphs, Dryads, Genii, etc., Semi-Gods or Goddesses. Of these, some are so near and familiar to men, that they are affected with human troubles. And in Denmark and Norway there are Daemons of a divers kind that are subject to the service of men, some of them are corporeal and mortal, whose bodies being generated perish, but they are of long life. This is the opinion of the Egyptians, of the Platonists, Proclus, Plutarch, Demetrius and Aemylius.

There are Daemons of this third sort as many Legions as there are stars in heaven. Athanasius saith that the numbers of good Daemons are thought to be 99 according to the Parable of the 100 sheep. Later Divines say that the number of good Angels transcends all human capacity, to which on the other side there are innumerable unclean spirits in this lower world as there are clean spirits in the upper world: under these they place a subterranean dark kind of Daemon, which the Platonics call deserting angels, the revengers of Impiety, bad daemons, wicked spirits, there are legions of them, and distinguished according to the names of the stars and Elements and parts of the world, some are Kings, Princes and Presidents, as *Clavicula Salomonis* doth inform. Porphyrius saith these daemons inhabit this Earth and there is no sort of mischief which they dare not perpetrate and delight to act all kinds of villainy.

Of the 28 Mansions of the Moon and of Their Strength and Virtue in Mundane Affairs

In the space of 28 days the Moon runs through the Zodiac and according to Alpharus, these mansions partake of divers properties and names from divers stars in the Eighth Sphere, whose powers and virtues they partake of. It is Rabbi Abraham's opinion that every one of these Mansions contains 12 degrees, 51 minutes and 26 seconds almost, whose names as well as their beginnings in the Eighth Sphere are these:

The First Mansion is called Alnath, that is the horns of Aries, the beginning thereof is from the head of Aries of the Eighth Sphere. It makes journeys prosperous but it creates discord. A good time to give physic, chiefly laxatives.

The Second Mansion is called Allothaim or Alboctia, that is the body of Aries, the beginning thereof is from the 12th degree of the same sign, 51 minutes, 22 seconds complete. This Mansion is good to find out treasure hid, to the keeping of captives, to go voyages, to sow or plant, but contrary to purge or vomit.

The Third is called Achaomazone, a rainy Mansion, or Pleiades. The beginning is from 25 degrees complete of Aries, minutes 42, 51 seconds. Good for navigation, hunting and the works of Alchemy.

The Fourth Mansion is called Aldebaran, that is the eye or head of Taurus, the beginning thereof is from the 8th degree thereof, minutes 34, seconds 17. This Mansion destroys and hinders buildings, fountains, wells, gold mines, and generates discord.

The Fifth Mansion is called Alchataya or Albachaya the beginning thereof is from the 21st degree of Taurus, 25 minutes, 43 seconds. It causeth a safe return from a long journey or voyage; good for instruction of scholars, confirms buildings, gives health and favour among persons of quality.

The Sixth Mansion is called Alhanna or Alchaia, that is a small star of great light, his beginning after the fourth degree of Gemini, 17 minutes and 9 seconds. It is good for hunting and besieging cities, a revenge to princes; destroys harvests and fruits and hinders the operation of physic.

The Seventh is called Aldimiach or Alarzach, that is to say, the arm of Gemini, and it begins from the 17th degree of Gemini, 8 minutes, 34 seconds and lasteth to the end of that sign. It brings gain and friendship, it is profitable for lovers, it destroys Magisteries, and this fourth part of the heavens is complete in these seven Mansions. And in like order and number of degrees, minutes and seconds, the remaining Mansions in the several quarters have their several beginnings that in the first sign of that quarter, three Mansions may have beginning in the other two signs, two Mansions in either.

And, therefore, the seven following mansions begin from the head of Cancer, whose names are Alnaza, or Anatrachia, that is, cloudy, to wit, in the Eighth Mansion. It causeth love and friendship, and the society of travellers, afflicts captives, holding them in prison.

The Ninth Mansion is called Archaam or Alchaph, that is, the eye of the Lion. It destroys harvests and travellers and makes discord amongst men.

The Tenth is called Algelioche or Algebh, that is, the neck or the forehead of Leo. It confirms buildings, gives love, favour and help against enemies.

The Eleventh Mansion is called Azobra or Ardaf, that is, the hair of the Lion. It is good for travellers and gain in merchandise and for redemption of captives.

The Twelfth Mansion is called Alzarpha or Azarpha, that is, the tail of the Lion. It gives prosperity to harvests and plantations but hinders navigators; but it is good for servants and captives and bettering their companions.

The Thirteenth Mansion is called Alhayre, that is, the wings of Virgo. It produceth friendship, gain, journeys, harvests, and deliverance of captives.

The Fourteenth is called Achuroth or Arimet, of others Azimeth or Alhumech, that is, Spica Virginis or Spica Volans. It avails to the love of married persons, to heal the sick, it profits navigators, but hinders such as travel by land. And in these Mansions is the second quarter of heaven complete. The other 7 Mansions follow, of which the first begins in the head of Libra.

The Fifteenth Mansion and the name thereof Agrapha or Algarpha, that is, covered or covered flying. It avails for extracting treasures, for digging wells. It causeth discord, divorce, and the destruction of houses and enemies, and hinders travellers.

The Sixteenth Mansion is called Azubene or Ahubene, that is, the horns of Scorpio. It hinders journeys and marriage, harvests and merchandise. It avails to the deliverance of captives.

The Seventeenth is called Alchil, that is, the Crown of Scorpio. It makes better cross fortune, makes love durable, confirms buildings and prospers navigators.

The Eighteenth is called Alchas or Altob, that is, the heart of Scorpio. It causeth discord, sedition and conjuration, against princes and powers, and to the revenge of enemies: but it delivers captives and makes good for buildings.

The Nineteenth Mansion is called Ablatha or Achala, of others, Hycula or Axala, that is, the tail of Scorpio. It is good to besiege cities and to take towns and to drive men away from those places, and to the destruction of navigators and perdition of captives.

The Twentieth Mansion is called Abnahaya, that is to say, a beam. It is good to tame wild beasts, to keep men in prisons, destroys the wealth of confederates, compels a man to come to any place.

The One and Twentieth is called Abeda or Albeldach, which is a desert. It makes for harvests, gain to buildings and travellers, and for making divorce. And in this Mansion the third quarter of heaven is completed. There remains the last seven Mansions completing the last quarter of heaven, whereof the first which is in order.

The Two and Twentieth beginning from the head of Capricorn, is called Savahaca or Zodeboluch or Zandeldona, that is a shepherd. It promotes the flight of servants and captives and to the healing of the sick.

The Twenty Third Mansion is called Sabadola or Zobrach, that is devouring, makes for divorce, for the deliverance of captives, and the healing of the sick.

The Twenty Fourth Mansion is called Sadabath or Chaderoad,

which is, the star of fortune, and avails for the good agreement of the married, for the victory of soldiers. It hurts the undertaking of Magisteries and hinders that they shall not be accomplished.

The Twenty Fifth Mansion is called Sadalabra or Sadalachia, that is, a Pavilion or Tent. It makes good for betraying or revenge, destroys enemies, confirms prisons and buildings, makes speedy messengers, makes for witchcraft, copulation and to the tying up for any member of a man that it shall not perform its office.

The Twenty Sixth mansion is called Alpharg or Phtagal Mocadon, that is hauriens primus. It makes for union and love of men, for the safety of captives, destroys prisons and buildings.

The Twenty Seventh is called Alcharya or Alhalgalmoad, that is hauriens secundus. Increaseth harvests, merchandise, gain, heals diseases; but hinders buildings, prolongs men in prisons, and helps to bring mischief on whom you will.

The Twenty Eighth Mansion is called Albothan or Alchalh, that is, fishes, increases harvests and merchandise, secures travellers through dangerous places, conduceth to the joy of wedlock, but keeps men in prison and causeth men to lose treasures.

And in these 28 Mansions of the Moon lie hid many secrets of the wisdom of the ancients, by which many miracles have been wrought in all things that are under the Circle of the Moon. And the ancients attributed to every Mansion his proper resemblance or Image or Seal and the Intelligences that governed, and they worked by their virtues divers ways.

Of the Images of the Mansions of the Moon

In the First mansion, for the destruction of any man, they made the image of a black man in an iron ring, clothed with a hair garment and girded, bearing on his right side a lance, and they sealed it in black wax, and fumigated it with liquid Storax and made an imprecation.

In the Second Mansion, against the anger of the prince, and for reconciliation, they made the Image of a King Crowned, and sealed it with white wax and Mastic and fumigated it with Lignum Aloes.

In the Third they made an Image in a silver ring, whose table was squared, and whose figure was a woman well clothed, sitting in a chair, her right hand lifted up above her head, and they sealed it and fumigated it with Moscho [Musk?], Camphor and an Aromatic hoof, this would give prosperity of fortune and all good.

In the Fourth Mansion, for revenge, separation and enmity, they sealed an Image in red wax of a Soldier sitting on a horse holding in his right hand a serpent, and they fumed it with red Myrrh and Storax.

In the Fifth, for the favour of Kings and Officials, and good reception, they made a seal in silver, bearing the head of a man. They fumigated it with Sandal.

In the Sixth Mansion, for increase of love between parties, they sealed in white wax two Images embracing one another, and fumed it with Lignum Aloes and Amber.

In the Seventh Mansion, to gain riches, make a Sigil of silver bearing the Image of a man well clothed, holding up his hands to heaven as if praying and supplicating, and fumigate it with good odours.

In the Eighth Mansion, to gain victory in war, they made the Image of an eagle of tin, having the face of a man, and they fumigated it with Sulphur.

In the Ninth, to help infirmities, they made a Sigil of lead bearing the Image of a man wanting his Virga and witnesses with his hands covering his eyes, and they fumigated it with Resin of the pine tree.

In the Tenth, to further childbirth and heal the sick, they made a sigil bearing the figure of the head of a Lion and fumed it with Amber.

In the Eleventh Mansion, to create a fear, reverence and veneration, they made a golden Lamen, the Image of a man riding upon a Lion, with his left hand holding him by the ear, and fumed it with sweet odours and Saffron.

In the Twelfth Mansion, for to cause a separation of lovers, they made in a seal of black lead, the Image of a Dragon fighting with a man, and fumed it with Lion's hair and Asafoetida.

In the Thirteenth Mansion, to cause concord and love after marriage, and to dissolve witchcraft when they copulate, they made both their forms in a seal, the man in red wax, the woman in white wax, embracing one another, fumigating it with Lignum Aloes and Amber.

In the Fourteenth Mansion, for divorce and separation of the man and the woman, they made in a seal the Image of a Dog biting his tail, and fumigated it with the hair of a black dog and a black cat.

In the Fifteenth Mansion, for gaining friendship and good will, they made the Image of a man in a seal sitting and reading letters and fumigated it with Frankincense and Nutmeg.

In the Sixteenth Mansion, to gain by merchandise, they made in a silver seal, the Image of a man sitting upon a chair holding a spear in his hand, and they fumigated it with sweet odours.

In the Seventeenth Mansion, against thieves and robbers, in an iron seal they made the Image of an ape, and fumed it with the hairs of an ape.

In the Eighteenth, against fevers and pains of the body, they made a seal in brass bearing the Image of the tail of a belly worm holding it above his head, and fumigated it with hart's horn. The same Sigil being buried caused all serpents and venomous creatures to quit that place.

In the Nineteenth Mansion, to make childbirth easy and to provoke the menstrua, they make in a seal of brass, an Image of a woman holding her hands upon her face, and they fumed it with liquid Storax.

In the Twentieth mansion, for hunting, they made in a seal of tin bearing the Image of Sagittarius, half a man and half a horse, and they fumed it with the head of a fox.

In the One and Twentieth Mansion, for the destruction of any thing, they made the Image of a man with a double forehead or countenance before and behind, and fumed it with Sulphur and a Lobster and laid it in a brass box.

In the Two and Twentieth, to secure fugitives, they made in an iron seal the Image of a man with winged foot, on his head wearing an Helmet, and they fumed it with quicksilver.

In the Three and Twentieth Mansion, to work the destruction and devastation of any thing or person, they made a seal of iron bearing the Image of a Cat having a Dog's head, and fumigated it with Dog's hair and buried it in a place where they designed to hurt any man.

In the Four and Twentieth Mansion, to the increase of flocks and cattle, they took the horn of that ram, bull, or goat or other beast which they would multiply, and made in an iron seal the Image of a woman suckling her child, and they hanged this seal on the neck of that beast which was the ringleader of the herd or flock.

In the Twenty Fifth Mansion, for the preservation of trees and plants, they made in a seal of the wood of a fig tree, the Image of a man planting, and they fumigated it with the flowers of the fig tree, and did hang it on the tree.

In the Twenty Sixth Mansion, to create love and favour, they made in a seal of white wax and Mastic, the Image of a woman washing and combing her hair, and fumigated it with sweet scent.

In the Twenty Seventh Mansion, to destroy fountains, wells, baths, they made of red earth the Image of a man winged, an empty vessel bored through which he held in his hands, and the Image being baked, they put into the vessel Asafoetida and liquid Storax, and buried them in a well, which they would destroy.

In the Twenty Eighth Mansion, to gather fishes together, they made in a brass seal, the Image of a fish, and fumigated it with the skin of a seafish, and cast it into the water wheresoever they would have the fishes gather together.

Moreover, with the foresaid Images they also did inscribe the names of the Spirits and their Characters, did Invocate and Imprecate them to do that which they desired to obtain.

Of Spirits Called Hobgoblins

These kind of spirits play mad pranks without doing any harm. They sometimes play on Gitterns and Jews Harps, and ring bells, and answer those that call them with laughter and merry gestures, so that those of the house come at last to be so familiar and well acquainted with them that they fear them not at all. But if they had free power to put in execution their malicious desire, we should find these pranks of theirs not to be jests but earnest indeed, tending to the destruction of body and soul.

Trasgosy gives some examples of frolics acted by Daemons to prove the truth of what is here asserted. I will at the end of these magical discourses relate some historical examples of the actions of spirits with men, and a wonderful but true history of a maiden that was enamoured of the Devil.

It is an opinion of great antiquity and averred by the learned that whensoever any man is possessed, the soul of some one that is dead should enter into him and speak within him. This is absurd, for though sometimes God permits the Souls departed, for some special causes to return unto the world, yet doth he not permit them to enter into a body where is another soul. For two reasonable souls can by no means abide in one body, so that there cannot be a greater error than this. For without doubt they are devils and not souls, as we may see by their casting forth, which is done by the virtue of holy and sacred words, at which time they use their utmost endeavour not to be constrained to go into places where they cannot exercise their malice. An example of him in Luke 8 possessed of a Legion of Devils, was delivered of them by our Saviour, by whose permission they entered a herd of swine, which threw themselves immediately down the rocks tumbling into the sea.

Psellus and Guadentius Merula show as the cause why the Devils are so desirous to enter into men's bodies, and can with such difficulty be cast out of them, making thereunto all resistance that they possibly may. The reason is this, that though the Devils are enemies unto men, yet they enter into their bodies not so much with will to do them hurt, as with a desire of a vital heat and warmness. For these spirits are such as inhabit the deepest and coldest planes, where the cold is so pure that it wantest moistness. So that they covet places hot and moist, searching all opportunities and occasions to enter into them so often as for some reasons which we understand not, God suffereth and permitteth them so to do.

And when they cannot enter into the bodies of men, they enter into the bodies of other creatures where willingly they detain themselves so long as they may, and through the violent strength which the body by their entry receiveth, happen those tremblings, shakings and forcible motions, which we see they use that are possessed.

This kind of Devils use the spirit of the patient as their proper instrument and with his tongue speak and utter what they list. But if they be such spirits as fly the light and dwell in the profundities of the Earth, as the last and utmost sort of those of the Earth, then they make the patient both deaf and dumb like a block without understanding, as though he were deprived of all his senses and forces which he had before. And this is the worst of all and with the greatest difficulty cast out.

The Difference between Witches and Enchanters

Enchanters are so called who publicly and openly have any agreement or Covenant with the Devil, by whose help they work things which are in appearance wonderful, entering into Circles they cause them to appear and speak, consulting with them using their favour and aid in all their works and many they make the Devil alone to do for them.

Witches are those which though they have familiarity and conversation with the Devil, yet the same is in such sort that they themselves scarcely understand the error wherewith they abuse themselves, using unknown signs, characters and other superstitions in which they secretly invoke the names of the Devils, using their aid and counsel. And because the Devil may the better bring them to his bias, he discloseth unto them some properties and virtues of roots, herbs and stones and other things, which have secret operations, mingling the one with the other, that is to say, that of Natural Magic with that of the Devil. But to conclude they may all be called Witches and Enchanters which with Natural Magic (which is the knowledge of those things whom Nature hath imparted these secret virtues), mingle signs, characters and words, using them though they may understand them not, in their Sorceries and Witchcraft.

The Devil Doth Sometimes Enter the Body of Unreasonable Creatures

This is verified by Scripture of the Devils that entered the herd of swine.

A memorable example I will here impart. There was a student in Guadaloupe that on an evening walking in the field saw a clergyman riding on a horse so lean and tired scarce able to stand on his feet; entertaining some discourse with him the traveller told him that he was bound for Granada which was 400 miles distant, the student being poor and having friends there, wished he had a horse to bear him company thither. The traveller being glad of company, importuned the student to get behind him on the croupe of his horse, at which the scholar laughing told him that his horse in respect of his leanness, seemed to be fitter for dog's meat than to carry two men at once on his back. "Well," quoth the clergyman, "if you know my horse as well as I do, you would not say so, for I assure you how ill favoured soever he look, there is not his fellow in the world, neither would I sell him for my weight in gold; and if you doubt of his ability to carry us both, get but up and you shall soon know the contrary." The student got up and this lean palfrey carried them away with such smoothness and so swiftly, that he thought he never rode pleasanter in his life and every foot his companion asked him what he thought of his lean beast, assuring him that he would not be tired or alter his pace though the journey were never so long. After they had ridden all night, at last the dawning of the day began to appear, and the student saw before him a goodly country full of gardens and pleasant trees, and not far off a very great city. Asking of the clergyman what country and city the same was, he said that they were within the precincts of Granada. Desiring him in recompense of his safe journey, not to utter this matter of him and his horse to any man living. The student thanked him and parted with him, but went to the town the most amazed man in the world thinking it impossible to finish a voyage of so many miles in one night unless there had been some devil within the horse, as most likely there was.

But this example is not strange, for the Devils lost not their nature, though they lost grace, then is the power and force which they have if they be in liberty and not restrained, like unto that of the good angels, and as the Angel carried by the hair the prophet Abucuck out of Jewry into the Den of Lions which was in Babylon where Daniel was; might the Devil likewise carry those so great a journey as I said. And in this manner do they carry those men and women called sorcerers and Hags whither they will themselves.

The Sorcerers and Hags are a lineage and kind of people which are expressly agreed and accorded with the Devil, holding and obeying him as their sovereign prince and master, and suffering themselves to be marked of him as his slaves, which marks they bear in one of their eyes fashioned like a Toad's foot by which they know and have notice one of another. For they have amongst themselves great companies and fraternities making often general meetings together, at which times they pollute themselves with all fifthiness, abominable villainies, beautiful lusts and Infernal Ceremonies, and always whensoever they meet so together, they do lowly homage and reverence to the Devil who most commonly appeareth to them in the figure of a great Ram Goat.

To prove the truth hereof I shall relate briefly what happened to a learned man in Spain recorded by the authors of *Malleus Malleficarum*. There was a learned man who suspecting a neighbour of his to be a Sorcerer entered into a league of friendship with him covering so finely his dissimulations, that the other was content to admit of him into the society he kept and that in so doing he should enjoy all the pleasures and contentments in the world, so it was agreed between them that at the next assembly of theirs he should go and make his covenant and confederation with the Devil, putting himself under his banner and protection. The day assigned being come and gone, after it was darkness, the sorcerer took the learned man out of the town and carried him along certain valleys and thickets where he had never been before though he knew the country round about very well, and in short space he thought that they had gone very far, coming at last into a plain field enclosed round about with mountains, where he saw a great number of people, men and women, that went up and down in great mirth, who all received him with great feast and gladness, giving him many thanks for that it had pleased him to become a member of their society, assuring him that there was no greater happiness in the world, than that which he should enjoy. In the midst of this field was a throne built very sumptuously in which stood a great and mighty Ram Goat, to whom at a certain hour of the night they all went to do reverence and going up certain degrees one after another, they kissed him in the foulest part behind. The learned man seeing an abomination so great, though he were by his companion thoroughly instructed how he should behave himself, could no longer have patience, but began to call unto God, at which very instant there came such a terrible thunder and tempest as though heaven and earth should have gone together, in such sort that he became for a time through great astonishment senselessly and without all judgment and understanding, in which sort he knew not himself how long he continued. But when he came to himself it was broad day, and he found himself among certain rough mountains so bruised and crushed as though he had scarcely any one sound bone in his body, and being desirous to know what this place might be wherein he was, coming down from those mountains to the plain country underneath, he found people so strangely differing in habit, custom and speech from those of his country, that he neither understood their language nor what course best to take to get home. But making a virtue of necessity, craving charity by signs and guiding himself by the Sun he took his way towards the West and was three years in his journey homewards, enduring by the way great hardships in so long travel to his home. As soon as he came home he certified the Magistrate what he had seen, accusing by name and surname divers persons which he had seen and known in that abominable assembly, who were apprehended, found guilty and executed.

You may read Alonso De Castra Cap. 16, *De Iusta Punito Haereticorum* who confirms what I have writ, and makes a difference between those Hags and Sorcerers and those Enchanters and Witches I mentioned before. For (saith he) these Hags and Sorcerers are agreed only with the Devil to the end that they might in this life enjoy all manner of delights and pleasures. The first time that they go to present themselves before him, and to do him homage they find him not in the likeness of a goat, but like a King of great and royal authority. They are all brought into his presence by other Devils in figure of Ram-goats, whom they call Martinets. Moreover, he saith that the reverence and homage which they do unto him, is not like that which we use unto princes, but in turning their shoulders and bowing down their heads as low as they can, and that he which is newly assumed into this brotherhood doth first with words wicked and abominable, blaspheme and renounce all the holy points and mysteries contained in our Catholic belief, vowing unto the Devil his faithful service for ever, with many other execrable ceremonies, vows and oaths which he there useth, which being accomplished, they mingle themselves together, and many devils with them in likeness of young gentlemen, and some of beautiful dames, where without shame or respect they fulfil in all abomination their filthy lust and beastly appetites. And of this company the greater part or in a manner all are women, as being through frailty and ignorance readiest to be deceived by the Devil and aptest thereunto through the lust of the flesh. And these women, saith he, are called Lamia and Stirges. For Lamia is a most cruel beast, which hath the heart of a woman and the feet of a horse; and Stirges is a bird that flieth by night, called a Screech Owl, makes great shrieking and noise. When she can get into any place where children are, doth suck out their blood and drink it. For which cause the Sorcerers are also called Stirges, because they work the same effect, sucking out the blood of men, when by any means they may, especially that of little children.

I will now add the two manners of ways by which the Sorcerers are present in general assemblies with the Devil. The one through the deceit of certain oils and ointments with which they anoint themselves, which depriveth them of their right soul, making them imagine that they are transformed into birds and beasts, deceiving not only themselves with this error but oftentimes also the eyes of others that behold and view them, for the Devil with deceitful appearance, formeth about them that phantastical body, which is also practised by sundry Enchanters, who so dazzle and deceive our sight, as did Circe and Medea, and others that used the art of Magic, turning and transforming men into brute beasts, to the seeming of all those which beheld them, though in truth it was nothing so. For as the philosopher Aristotle saith, it is impossible to change one shape into another. And the Council of Aquilon useth these words—"Whosoever doth affirm that any creature may be transformed into any other thing better or worse, or take any other shape than that in which it was of God created, is an infidel."

But the Sorcerers and Sorceresses, though they find the manner wherewith they are deceived and abused, yet they take it well and give consent thereunto, thinking themselves in these imaginations to be transported with great swiftness into those parts which they desire, and verily do see and find themselves in action of these, those things which to their phantasy are represented.

The other kind of going to the assemblies, and transporting them to far places with such swiftness, is really and truly by help of the Devils, upon whom they sometimes ride in likeness of goats, sometimes they anoint themselves with other ointments, whose operation maketh them think they are fowls and fly in the air, when indeed they are carried by the Devils. This is verified by all authors both ancient and modern, that the Devil can in very short space, and as it were in an instant, transport these sorcerers into marvellous far regions. For he which had power to carry our Saviour Christ (with reverence I speak it) out of the desert and to set him on the top of a pinnacle on the Temple, and from there to convey him to a high mountain where he might view and discover a great part of the world, can far more easily transport a man or woman through the air.

Much more I find in Alonso de Castra to prove what I have writ. He allegeth the authority of Paulus Grillandus in his treatise of heretics.

Malleus Maleficarum telleth of a woman, a sorceress, who affirmed obstinately before the Commissioners, that she could come and go bodily whither she list in short space though she were never so fast imprisoned and the way never so far off, that for trial they presently caused her to be shut up in a chamber and willed her to go to a certain house and learn what was there done and to bring them relation thereof, the which she promised to do. After she remained a while alone the Commissioners caused the door to be suddenly opened and entering the chamber found her lying stretched out on the ground as if dead. One of them curious to see if she had any feeling or no, took a candle and with the flame thereof scorched one of her legs, but seeing no sign of motion in her he left her and departing out of the chamber caused the door to be fast locked again. Presently upon which she came forth, telling the Commissioners that she had gone and come with great travail, declaring unto them the marks and tokens of all such things as they asked, obstinately declaring that she had been present, and viewed the scene with her eyes. Whereupon they asked her if she felt no grief in one of her legs. She answered that since her coming back it grieved her very sore. Then laid they before her the grossness of the error wherewith she was abused, and told her what they had done unto her in manner as before, which she truly perceiving fell down upon her knees and craved pardon upon promise of her repentance and amendment of life.

Lucius Apuleius and Grinaldus declare how sorcerers or witches are able to change not only their own but other men's shapes, also as Circe and Medea did, and partly through natural magic, that is the knowledge of the virtues of herbs, stones, oils and ointments, whose properties are by the devils revealed unto them and partly through the mere help of the Devil employing there in his whole power for the better binding and assuring them to be perpetually his.

Zoroaster, Lucius Apuleius, Apollonius Tyaneus have been of old famous or rather infamous in the world by their sorcery and necromancy, with many others whom historians thought unworthy to commend to posterity.

Another sort of them called Charmers, who have a particular gift of God to heal the biting of mad dogs, and to preserve people and cattle from being endamaged by them. Franciscus Victoria saith that they have the wheel of St. Katherine, in the roof of their mouths, who though they may do great help in such like matters, yet to hear their prayers and Conjurations and clownish phrases would move anyone to laughter. They are a base forlorn people of ill example in their life and boast sometimes of more than they can accomplish and some of them will creep into a red hot oven without danger of burning.

Pliny writeth alleging the authority of Crates Pergamonas that there is in Hellespont a kind of men called Ophrogens, who with only touching heal the wounds made by serpents. Varro saith that in the same country there are men which with their spittle heal the biting of serpents. Isigonus and Nymphodurus affirm that there is in Africa a certain people whose sight causeth all things to perish which they intentively fix their eyes on, so that the trees wither and the children die, and therewith more might be wrote of this head.

Anthonia de Florencia
His Opinion Why the Devil Suggesteth Evil Thoughts To Us in Our Sleep

He represents to our phantasy those things in which we take delight and such as are pleasing to our humours and appetites, especially making us dream lascivious dreams and tempting us so far with filthy and carnal lusts, that he provoketh us oftentimes to pollutions. To others he represents in their sleep great treasures and riches, to the end that waking they might be stirred with desire of them, and have their thoughts and imagination busied about them, leaving matter of better meditation. But his malice is not always herewith contented for sometimes it tendeth further, provoking us in our sleep to commit follies, whereby we may lose both body and soul at once.

A wonderful but true narrative I will here in short declare concerning one Tapia, who had so strange a condition in his sleep, that he arose divers nights sleeping out of his bed, and went up and down the house from place to place without waking. For which cause, to prevent danger, his servants used to set up a shallow tub of water by his bedside, that when he was troubled with that passion, if he touched the cold water he would presently awake. His servants one night forgot to set this vessel by the bedside. The season being very hot, he arose sleeping out of his bed with great agony to go swimming in the river, and casting about him a cloak over his shirt, he went out of his chamber, unbolted the door of the house, hastened to the riverside, coming to the town's end he met with another companion who seemed glad of the opportunity to go with him into the river. So was Tapia, who putting off his cloak and shirt, and ready to enter into the water, the other fell a scoffing and jeering at him as at one that knew not how to swim, which he taking an ill part, because he was therein very expert, answered in choler that he would swim with him on what wager he pleased. So the other forthwith went up to the top of a high bridge that crossed over the same river, he stripped himself naked and threw himself down headlong into the water, the river running in that place very swift and dangerous. Where swimming up and down in the main stream, he called upon Tapia, bidding him to do the like. But Tapia, disdaining to be less courageous than the other went likewise up to the top of the bridge and threw himself down in the same place the other had done before him, till which time still remaining fast asleep, his feet were no sooner in the water, but he awakened presently, where finding himself plunging in midst of the rough stream, though in great amazement, yet with all the speed he could, he scrambled forth earnestly calling on his companion that brought him thither with him, thinking assuredly that there was a man swimming with him indeed, but having passed with great difficulty the danger of the stream, after long calling and looking about him, when he could neither see nor hear any man make answer he began to mistrust, that this matter proceeded by the crafty illusion and deceit of the Devil who (as he truly thought) endeavoured by the subtle practice and enticement to destroy in his sleep both his body and soul.

Of Presaging by Dreams

The Light of God and Nature contradict not Daniel and others by dreams foretold natural things, for the sidereal spirit was so disposed, Joseph by the help of this star interpreted the fat and lean oxen to show the fertility and difficulty of provision. This being a natural cause, it was interpreted by the Light of Nature. By dreams many things diverse ways are to us revealed not only by a star, but by an Angel of God.

To make easy one of Enoch's Tables I shall briefly set down the cause and interpretation of all dreams under these heads:

1 Concerning Joseph's Oxen
2 The Graecian Horse
3 Dreams merry jocose
4 Serious Dreams
5 Riotous Dreams
6 Sick Dreams
7 Dreams of fortune
8 Dreams of misfortune

Concerning Joseph's oxen this tenet will be verified that so often you dream of an Ox, so often the year may be judged, for the nature the Ox is of, the like the year will prove. There was a certain diviner that dreamed of future riches. To this his constellation propounded 15 lean oxen and at last one fat ox. Thence he concluded that the 15 lean oxen were given him that he should sell them when they were fatted. In the meantime he was forced for 15 years to wander up and down in a miserable starving condition. But in the sixteenth year he happened to enjoy a fat ox, that is to say a rich wife. With this wife he lived one year and then died. The lesser cattle some signify a quarter of a year, some a month, some a week, some a day, and some an hour.

By the Graecian Horses are meant that Man's constellation in his own thought is of that great power, that he may have the help of a starry spirit in his dream without the help of an Elementary body. This Astral Body hath the force to infect with poison, make sick, blind, puffing up, aspiring and beating, and that in an instant, and afterwards to return to his Elementary body. For it is plain that by so strong an imagination, the ancients in battle, by force of the astral body prevailed against the enemy so that some of a sudden were taken paralytic in their bodies, no natural cause concurring, some deprived of their sight, some made leprous, and some almost strangled, and many other mischiefs like those are inflicted which cannot be cured in a long time.

The power of an astral spirit is great in the forming of dreams and their fatality. As for vain ludicrous dreams whose interpretation is doubtful, you must know that in the sidereal spirit there is no perfection, but tends to the delusion that the dream will prove happy, though in the end it will not prove so. There are many dreams that prove true to the finding out of treasure, success in marriage, climbing up to honour, as also forerunners of sorrow, poverty and all hardships, according to everyone's predestination and the benevolence of the stars. And none can deny that dreams, have their practice by which starry bodies are compelled that they should reveal anyones intention. The reason of this practice is wonderful, neither is it obvious or received of everyone, for it causeth that the stars manifests by what is asked, and this is done, whilst the Imagination, trust, hope and charity, and the persuasion of the starry spirits is so far looked into as nothing is able to deny it. And though prayer may indeed be directed to God, yet it is not of the soul but from the light of Nature. Therefore, that practice is placed upon the foundation of imagination. love, hope, expectation, and serious friendship.

The astral spirit hath speculation; of great moment is speculation, from thence flows good and evil. From speculation arises an Usurer, whoremaster, dicer, blasphemer, etc., from the same arise what is good. The invention of sciences whether mechanical or not is due to speculation, so is Alchemy, but the Astral spirits before a due time learn nothing. Nothing can be speculated but what is found and comprehended by Astral spirits.

Our mind governs a star, so that a star follows the mind and with it is reconciled. As if saffron be cast into water, all the water waxeth yellow, so a star comparatively like saffron penetrates man and with man is united. A star is the tincture of speculation of the mind, that is of all things of man. Because therefore a star is the tincture, man is the body that is tinged. Let none admire that a star many ways operates in man. But there are peculiar stars which have a regard and do govern beasts but their influence and constellation is of a different nature from man's.

It is therefore practical that man should incline himself towards the stars and be joined with them, that so he may compel and change all things to its own essence. Therefore as to the practical part of divination we determine that it finds out great arts, sciences and workmanships. And it were good that worldly men should receive such a Light of Nature, and not busy themselves with intimate phantasies, or study to deceive themselves or others, but embrace the genuine star, and obey the same which will tend to the recreation and welfare of his earthly body, without any loss or prejudice to his Soul or his Image.

Behold how the Stars, Angels and Genii communicate their virtues in dreams, how they come down with their influential power by the beams of the planets to the Earth by the figures of Astromancy and Geomancy to the bodies of men in their dreams. Many of the ancient learned Hebrews, Greeks and Latins, have handled the subject of dreams, but with so little assurance, that amongst a thousand significations, there are hardly two true, having no more experience for what they advance than conjecture and imaginations, whereof they have made large volumes, which have rendered them that studied them more anxious and perplexed than they were before for their dreams. But they are deceived though learned, not knowing that a thousand dreams which possess the spirit of man every night are nothing but a remembrance of his former actions; the which thing is common to him with the beasts, and that the occupation which the person thought most concerned his life and livelihood, is that which represents itself every night. Which Claudian hath represented in these verses:

Omnia quae sensu volvuntur vota diurno,
  Pectore sopito reddit amica quies.
Venator sua fesso tororum membra reponit,
  Mens tamen ad sylvas et sua lustia redit.

Judicibus lites, aurigae somnia currus,
      Unaque nocturnis mota cavetur equis.

Which in effect is no more but this:
      The Hunter, Lawyer, Carter all repent,
      The sense of what hath past the day forespent.

That which Antiquity thought divine in dreams was indeed nothing but folly, and that in this case, there is no difference between a man and a beast, for Solomon the wisest that ever has said. That the ends of the sons of men, and the end of beasts, is the same thing as to them, as the one dies so do the others, and they have all the same spirit, and a man naturally is no more than a beast, for all is vanity, all goes to the same place, all is dust, and all shall return into dust. Who is it that knows that the spirit of the children of men ascends up on high, and the spirit of the beast descends under the earth? For who can bring it back to see what was become of it? If this be doubtful who will attribute divinity to so many sottish visions dreamed by gross people. If a thousand figures are seen by a rustic in his sleep even so it is with a labouring beast; if the one chafes the other will show it is angry, all their passions are alike. Although dreams are equal to them with us, yet Man hath something more than is ordinary to beasts, some dreams being to him the forerunners of some fortunes or misfortunes which follow him the day after they have been seen and dreamt, and sometimes for a longer date.

There are 73 various dreams I find recorded by the ancient Cabalists, Merubalists and Massorets which are easily understood by those who know the temperament of those that have dreamed them and not otherwise. You must also know the day of the Moon, and the hour of the night they were dreamed in. I shall hereafter write a particular discourse on this subject of dreams, wherein I shall discover the errors of Artemiderus, Cardan and Nephius in their resolution of dreams. I shall only at this time add a few corollaries on this magical head and proceed further to the doctrine of the Nymphs, Sylphs, etc.

Dreams are either Divine or human.

Divine dreams without doubt are most certain, but be cautious to consider what dreams are properly Divine and what are not, for sometimes Satan transforms himself into an Angel of light. Divine dreams are tried by examining them by the rule of the known word of God. The Devil imitates God in dreams, creeps into the minds of foolish and improvident people who sometimes are possessed with enthusiasms from heaven. Abhor the dotings of fanatic people though they pretend never so much to derive them from heaven.

Next to divine dreams are the Angelical which may be believed if they agree with the Divine. But Diabolical dreams are to be detested, by which the heathens of old, and of late the Manichaeans, Pelagians, Monks and fanatic persons being deceived, were the authors and defenders of many horrible false doctrines. And it being granted that sometimes that the devil may know casual events, yet he often deceives the Magicians as to the true signification of things to come. The Conimbricensian Philosophers have written a large volume of this doctrine, and they charge Augustine, Damascenus, and Thomas Aquinas with it.

Human dreams which have no other but natural causes, and happen to men ordinarily as they sleep are either physical or common. The physical dreams are those which by the agitation of the humours, and disposition of the temperament, do by certain signs, nay sometimes even material and efficient causes discover unto the physician the more certain of constitution of the patient. These may be observed without impiety or atheism, to the end that more fortunate medicines may be provided for the sick. So a certain wrestler dreamed that he was plunged in a cistern of blood, and that he should hardly deliver himself thence. Accordingly to this dream, the physicians knowing it proceeded from an exuberance of blood, having taken away what abounded, diverted the danger he was in. Galen mentions another who dreaming that one of his legs became dead as a stone, a while after became paralytic in that leg.

Common dreams are those that proceed from compound causes; and they are true or false or equivocal. Many things in dreams may be rightly interpreted, yet many times may not happen accordingly. Hence it was so many Kings and Princes have miserably perished by this kind of dream.

So Cambyses dreaming that his crown touched the heaven, and that he sat in his brother Smerdis' royal seat, was to him the signification of death. Many dreams are ambiguous of a double sense uncertain and doubtful. One told a Conjector that he had dreamed he was turned into an Eagle. He answered, thou shalt overcome, for there is nothing swifter or more violent than that bird. But says Antiphon to him, dost thou not see thyself overcome, for that bird pursuing and chasing others is ever the last itself.

Of many Dreams there are but a few have there true events, especially in melancholy persons. Read Poucher *Lib. de Divinatione per somnium*. A certain man told a Conjector that he had dreamed he saw an egg hanging by a string of his bed. The Conjector answers that there was a treasure hid under his bed. He searches and finds a parcel of Gold compassed with Silver. He sent the interpreter what Silver he thought fit. But says the other, will you give me more of the yolk? For that doth as well signify the Gold as the white does the Silver.

Many holy persons have the society of the Guardian Genius by which they have the apprehension and knowledge of the death of their friends and kindred, either before or after they are dead by certain monetary dreams, or by a strange and unusual restlessness within themselves, though they be a thousand leagues distant, and they commonly dream of hair, or of eggs, or of teeth all mingled together with earth, a little before the death of any friend or relation. All which manifestly demonstrate the power of the Angels of Astromancy and Geomancy when they are united, and how Superiors and Inferiors communicate to man.

Having thus compendiously laid down the various opinions of philosophers both ancient and modern as to dreams of all sorts with a short explanation thereof, leaving the larger exposition to a particular treatise I shall hereafter set forth, if God spare me life and health to complete the same. I shall in the next place discourse of Nymphs, Sylphs, Pigmies, Salamanders, and other spirits, in order to the better understanding one of Enoch's Tables which is full of obscurity and darkness. This part of Magic is an Arcanum of great value though mysterious.

Of Nymphs, Sylphs, Pygmies and Salamanders, with Other Spirits

There is a light in man which is above the light of Nature. This light causeth him to search and learn and experiment supernatural things. Nature itself gives a light by which, as from a proper light the same may be known. For man is somewhat more than Nature, for he is both Nature, a spirit and an Angel, he hath the property of all three. How great is the dignity of man, he searcheth hell and heaven. In this discourse, I shall set forth created things beyond the knowledge of the light of Nature. Here are four sorts of spiritual men, to wit, Nymphs, Sylphs, Pigmies and Salamanders, to which are added Giants, Melusines, and Mons Veneris, and what are like them. All which we see not from Adam's progeny, but another sort of Creature, divers and separated from men and all living creatures, though they converse with us, and children be born of them.

I shall observe this method. First, lay down their creation and what they are. Secondly, their country and habitation, where they live and what government they have. Thirdly, how they appear among us, mingle themselves and cohabit with us. Fourthly, what miracles they act, as we read of Melusines, Mons Veneris and others. Fifthly, the generation of Giants, their original and end, nothing from Scripture as to their nature can be found, except some few testimonies of the Giants, the cause whereof is founded in this, that their works appear in verity. If we believe there is Magic and consider its original from that foundation, these matters may be known, for the writers of the Old and New Testaments treated of those things which concerns the welfare of the soul towards God, which hinders not this our philosophy. There is nothing created which wants its mystery. We find many wonderful things done in the Old Testament, which none can expound except he be instructed by the New Testament.

In the next place, consider what the Spirit is, what the Soul. Also the Spirit of these is flesh, and the flesh Spirit.

Flesh is two-fold, flesh from Adam and not from Adam. Flesh from Adam is gross, because earthy, but what flesh is not from

Adam, it is subtle, not fit to be bound or comprehended, 'the flesh of Adam cannot penetrate walls'. The difference lies from two offspring, that is, descending from two parents, and are in themselves, as the Spirit and Man. The spirit penetrates all walls, nor can be excluded from anything, but so is not man, who may be excluded.

But these subtle Creatures do differ in this from spirits, that they have blood, flesh and bones, beget children, speak, eat, drink, walk. Spirits do none of these. They are like spirits in agility, they are like men in generation, species and eating, and therefore they are men bearing the nature of both spirit and man, which in them is one.

Iamblichus saith, they are not men, because they walk spiritually; they cannot be spirits, because they eat, drink and have flesh and blood; they are therefore a peculiar Creature, and from their double nature they are made one mixture as any compounded matter of sweet and sour, or like two colours under one species. Man hath a Soul, a Spirit hath not, but the Creature is either and yet hath not a soul. Nor is it like a Spirit; a Spirit dies not, but a Creature dies; it hath not a Soul, it is not like a Man. Christ died not for those that are not of Adam's race. They beget children like themselves not us. They are prudent, rich, poor, fools, as we who are of Adam. And proceeding not from Adam, have not the Image of Man.

As to the nature of these Creatures that are not of Adam's race. They are men and people, dying with Animals, walking with Spirits, eating and drinking with men, that is to say, as cattle so they die, nothing remaining, and there is neither water nor fire that hurts them, as being spirits, neither can any one be able to shut them in as spirits. Their propagation is like to that of men, obtaining all their nature. They are obnoxious to human diseases and health, and use not the medicines of the land from which man was made, but the medicine wherein they live. They die as men but after the death of beasts, their flesh like other flesh putrefies, their bones like other bones perisheth, no footstep left. Their manners, gestures, speech, wisdom, are all human, either vicious or virtuous, gross or subtle, better of worse. They differ in themselves either in form or species, as other men. They live with men after the same law, eating the fruits of their own hand's labour, spinning and weaving their own garments, handling all things by a certain reason, governing with wisdom, administering Justice, for although they are animals, yet are all endued with human reason, only they have no souls. Therefore, they want the judgment of serving God, to walk in his ways, because they want a soul. Therefore, as animals act honestly in their life by an innate principle, so do they. But in reason, they overcome all other animals, and as man is next to God on earth above all Creatures, as to understanding and gifts, so they are next to man among all animals, and for this cause may be esteemed men. Neither are they destitute of any thing than the nature of a Spirit and the Soul of a Man—a peculiar and wonderful work of Creation, surpassing all things that can be considered.

Of their Habitation

Their habitation is divers, varying according to the Four Elements. They that live in the Water are called Nymphs; those that inhabit the Air are called Sylphs; those that are in the earth are called Pigmies; those that are in the Fire are Salamanders. These are the usual names, yet some will call watery men Undines, and airy men Sylvestres, and earthy men Gnomes, and fiery men Vulcans rather than Salamanders.

But if we describe their regions. Let their parts be divided, the Nymphs have no commerce with the Pigmies, nor they with them, and so among the Sylvestres and Salamanders every one hath his peculiar habitation; and here we may see the wonderful works of God who made no element void without a miracle contained in it. Consider their four Regions wherein they differ, as to their habitation, persons, essence and nature, and yet are more conformable to man than to one another.

We, the Sons of Adam, do stand and walk in the air, no otherwise than a fish in the waves, neither can we want air no more than a fish can want water, for as a fish lives in the water, and water is to it in the place of air, in like manner to a man is air instead of water; and so every Creature inhabits and walks in his own element. By this example you may understand, that the Undines inhabit the waters which serves them as air serves us. And as we admire that they live in the water, so they admire that we live in the air. The same reason may serve for the Gnomes who inhabit in the mountains, whereof the air and Chaos is their earth. For in the Chaos everything lives that is inhabit therein, walks therein, stands therein. But the Earth is only a Chaos to the Gnomes, for they pass through solid walls, stones and rocks, as spirits do, and therefore all these things are only to them a Chaos, that is, nothing. As the air hinders not us in our walking, even so the earth nor mountains nor stones, hinder the Gnomes, and with as much ease as we pierce the air, even so they pierce stones and rocks, for such things are to them a Chaos which is not so to us. As the Chaos is more gross, so the Creature is more subtle, as Man hath a subtle Chaos, therefore he is more gross. According to the condition of the Inhabitants so the Chaos varies in nature and property as to walking.

The Four Elements, then, is their habitation and their Chaos, and as we live in the air without damage, so they live in their Chaos, they are neither choked, strangled or burnt. For there are no such things but air to these Creatures which inhabit in them. For water is the air of the fish. If the fish is not choked, the Undine is not choked. What reason is for the water, the same is for the earth. The earth is the air of the Gnomes, therefore they are not strangled in it. They want not our air no more than we want theirs. So the air of the Salamanders is fire, so our air to us is air. But the Sylvestres are next to us, if indeed they are conversant with our air; but before others they die most like to us. For in the fire they are burnt, and so are we: in the earth they are strangled, and so are we. Therefore, every one remains sound in his own Chaos, but in another he dies. God is wonderful in his works.

But now to say something of the food of the Creatures. You must know, that every Chaos hath a double sphere, to wit a heaven and an earth, no otherwise than as we men walk in the earth, but the earth and heaven supply us food, and the Chaos as a medium lies between these two. So, therefore, we in the middle of these two spheres and little globe are nourished. In like manner they that inhabit in the water have the earth for their ground, and the water for their Chaos, and the heaven even to the water belonging, and also they that live in the middle of the heaven and earth, and therefore the water is their Chaos, but their habitation is agreeable to nature. So we must judge of the Gnomes, whose ground or earth is water, Chaos is earth, and the heaven is a sphere; that is the Earth stands in the water. But now the earth is to them a Chaos, and water is the ground, after this manner by these things is their aliment produced. The Sylphs are like unto men, and after their manner do live off the fields and herbs of the woods. The ground of Salamanders is the earth, and fire is the Chaos. So their food comes from the earth and fire, and the Constellation is from the air their heaven. But now for their eatables and drinkings. Water is drunk by us or satiates us, but not so the Gnomes, nor Nymphs, nor the other two. For as water quenches our thirsts, so there is another sort of created water for them, which we can neither see nor can find out. It is necessary they should drink, but that kind of drink which in their world is drunk. In like manner it is needful they should eat, but it is such sort of food which their world affords. This is certain that their worlds hath a peculiar property no otherwise than our own World hath.

As to their clothing, they have their clothing and hide their privates, but not after our fashion but their own, for they are modest as becomes men. Also they have their Orders, their Magistrates, as bees who have their king, or as the wild geese who have their leader. Neither live they according to the order of human laws, but according to the laws of their homebred nature. Their labour is like ours according to the nature of that world wherein they live. He that gave sheep's wool to us, the same gave them wool. God is able not only to create those sheep who are known to us, but otherwise such of foods in the fire, water, in the earth. The same God not only clothes them, but he clothes the Gnomes and Nymphs, Salamanders and Sylphs; they are all under God's protection, and they are all clothed and sustained by Him.

They sleep, rest, watch as we do. The Gnomes have the earth which is their Chaos, but this to them is air, not as it is earth to us, from thence it follows that they see by the earth, as we see by air. Lastly, they have the Sun and Moon and all the firmament before their eyes, as we have. In the like manner, the Undines have water for their Chaos. But water doth not intercept the Sun from them, but as we receive the Sun by the air so they receive it by the water. After the same manner, the Vulcans by their fire. Moreover, as the Sun irradiates us on the earth and makes it fruitful, so it makes them. So it is evident with them that the Summer, Winter, Day, night, and the like flourishes with them. As rain, snow, etc., is common with us, so it is with them. They are equally afflicted with pests, fevers, pleurisy and other diseases from heaven, as we are, but as to God's Judgment in the Resurrection, they are animals not men.

As to their person, the Undines, as well men as women, have the stature of a man. The Sylvestres have not that form, but are more sharp, grosser and longer than the others. The Gnomes are humble, about a span long. The Salamanders are oblong, slender and dry, but their seal and places are in the Chaos, as we said. The Nymphs inhabit the water that they may seize on men washing or riding. The Gnomes inhabit in a mountain Chaos. Hence it is that there are found around chambers and the like in the earth built and furnished. The Nymphs have the like lodgings. In like manner the clamour of the Salamanders is heard in the mountains of Etna, where they build lodgings, which are discovered in the conflagration of the Elements. They have all things common in our habitations, according to the property of their arcana. Certain documents are found in metal mines and waters, and Etna, where the Vulcans chiefly discover themselves. More might be added as to their money, their payments, their manners, etc.—shall be hereafter at large explained, when I shall deal with a History of the actions and manners of the Rosy Crucians.

After what manner these Creatures appear to us and are beheld of us

All Creatures that ever God created have manifested themselves to man, for God to this end manifested the Devil to man, that he should have knowledge of Him. In the like manner, the knowledge of Spirits and Soul, the Angels (were manifested) to men that they should know and believe that these Angels were from God whom they serve. But apparitions of this kind are seldom made but when something is to be confirmed and that we may learn how admirable and stupendous are the works of God, and to confirm the verity of the Holy Scriptures, and to certify us that such Creatures subsist in the Four Elements which seem wonderful in our eyes, and these Creatures converse with men and shall talk with them and the like, and that we may be better documented as concerning the Nymphs, they are not only seen of us, but they copulate and bear children. In the like manner, the Pigmies are not only seen of men, but talk with them and receive money of them and suffer the like passions as we do. And it is known that the Sylphs do negotiate and travel with men. Lastly, the Vulcans or Aetneans have appeared to men as we shall hereafter demonstrate. Furthermore, their appearance is by divine Judgment. As God sends us an Angel for our help and after that takes him away, so the Nymphs go out of their water and come to us, offer themselves to our service, negotiate with us, deal with us, then depart and return to their water, and all this for the sake of man, that he may better contemplate the divine works, but these men are only animals without a mind. From whence it comes that they copulate with men in Matrimony, that an Undine marries a man from Adam, takes care of all his courtesies in a familiar way, and bears children, and you must know that these children coming from Adam's race by the father, have a soul that partakes of eternity, and the wife after she is married receives a soul from God, and after the example of other women she is redeemed by God. This may be proved by many instances, that these Creatures of themselves are not eternal, but if they are joined with men by matrimony they are made eternal, and so after the manner of men they receive a soul. God created them so like men and conformable to man's nature in all things that nothing could be more like. So that copulation is the cause of the soul and salvation of these Nymphs, in like manner as Man's league with God and God's Covenant made with Man is the cause why he enters the Kingdom of God. If this league or Covenant were not, what would the Soul profit us? Truly nothing. Furthermore, there are two that are accounted spirits, to wit, the Pigmies and the Aetneans, not such Creatures as they appear like splendour and a spectrum. But you must know that they are flesh and blood as man is, although they be nimble, swift as spirits; they know all things past, present, and to come, occult from the eyes. In these things they serve men by revealing and forewarning. They have reason common with men, if they receive a soul. They have knowledge and the Intellect of Spirits, understood of those things that belong to God. They have great endowments; they lead and allure men to try these things of them, and we must believe that God brought forth these creatures that we might learn how great things God can work by his Creatures.

We have hitherto spoken of the Nymphs who come out of the water to us and in the banks of rivers where they inhabit, sometimes they are taken sitting and after the said manner are copulated.

But the Sylphs are grosser than those and know not how to speak, though they have a tongue and other things necessary for speech.

Of Gnomes, Etc.

The Gnomes have the same speech as the Nymphs, but the Aetneans speak nothing, though they are able to speak, although hardly and rarely.

The Nymphs go forth in a human habit and countenance, and appetite.

The Sylphs so appear like men, but they are false and fearful, and have no substance.

The Gnomes are like men, but they are short like dwarfs, sometimes equal to a middle sized man.

The Aetneans show themselves in a fiery habit and essence. These verily are those of which men talk of—In this house walks a fiery man or spirit, this burning soul wanders, etc.—as spirits of this kind are often seen. In meadows and grounds they appear like burning chips or brands running up and down and cause men to go out of their way. Such are the Vulcans. But we find these not to converse with men, by reason of the force of their fire, but they are often found among witches and with them to copulate. The Devil wanders with these and makes use of them to betray men. Without these fiery men conversation is dangerous, because for the most part they are possessed in whom the Devil rageth to the great damage of mankind. But sometimes the Devil enters into the Gnomes and serves them. In like manner the Devil lets himself into the Sylphs, chiefly their females, conversing with them in the woods and then copulates. Their births prove leprous, scabby, itchy, are incurable. These sorts of spirits commerce with men. They retain the nature of spirits as to their vanishing. Let him that take heed that hath a Nymph for his spouse, that he come not at the water, or hurt her in the water. In like manner, he that hath a Pigmean, let him not molest her in those places where she can separate. So strictly are men bound that without a cause they cannot separate from them, and this is wont to be in those places from which they go forth. And, therefore, a Nymph except she be upon the water, she cannot vanish away from her husband if she be provoked, in other places she may be kept. So also the Gnomes, if

they be once employed in our services, they are compelled to keep
to their covenant and perform those things required, and if the
promises be kept honestly on both sides then they remain true,
constant and faithful in their office, chiefly in gathering together
money. For the Gnomes abound in money, which they coin themselves. Which you shall so receive. He hath that of the spirit
whatsoever he wishes to have. For the Gnome gives him any
certain sum of money he desires and it is good current money. After
this manner they give money to many men in the Caverns of
mountains, that thence they may again depart. And so they buy
with a price the departure of men. All these things are done by God's
ordinance.

We have declared hitherto how these men come to us. It
remains that we explain after what manner they again depart from
us, or who are conversant with us. First, therefore, when they
copulate with men, they beget children, and when they are moved
to anger at men upon the water, then of a sudden throw themselves
into the water, nor are they found again. When, therefore, she thus
falls into the water she forsakes her husband and children, the
wedlock nevertheless remains entire, for you must know that in
regard of such a matrimonial that she will appear at the Last
Judgment, nor is she separated from that very soul, but attends the
same and expects due reward. For though, indeed, she remains a
Nymph she is compelled to act the same as soul and league
requires. In the meantime though they are disjoined from one
another, nor do not again meet together excepting at what time the
husband shall wed another wife. For then the Nymph returns and
brings death to the husband, as many times hath been observed.

After the same manner the Syrens are bred, living upon the
waters, rather then in the waters. These differ not from fishes, are
virgins but differ from the form of women in their lower parts.
These bring forth nothing but are monsters, no otherwise than if a
monstrous man should be born of two true men. Put the case that
Nymphs should produce themselves as men do, if they beget a
monster, they beget Syrens swimming on the waters, which these
parents eject, nor tolerate with themselves. Hence there are beheld
in divers shapes, as we do find it falls out in divers monsters. Nor

are the Nymphs alone the only cause of our wonder, but the Syrens which far exceed men by their various gestures. Some do sing, other play on the pipe, others act other things.

From the Nymphs are generated Moncks, which is a kind of monster. These represent a Monck both in species and form. They are like unto men, are found in like places, descend from men, that is, have their generation from Nymphs, Gnomes and the like. God himself works wonderful things in his creatures. So a comet from other stars hath his birth, as a certain monster, nor hath it a natural course as a star, but looked upon as a prodigy.

To this example are referred the monsters of the Sea, proceeding from the Nymphs, they are Comets, and of God manifested, that we may learn in his wonderful works. But because in very many Charity waxes cold, many such things are neglected, the greatest part of men are so given to usury, their own profit to dice and drinking, etc. But turn your eyes to these monsters, you shall become such after death, observe therefore admonition and take heed to your selves.

But why do these Nymphs ensnare men? You must know that men of this kind manifest themselves, and meet in one place, where they may live together, and have the familiarity of men which they studiously covet. For flesh and blood greatly loves flesh and blood. Many amongst them are wives to men. These are few, they are numerous. Which is the cause they hunt after and catch at other men. From these men there arises a gathering together and conversation which they call Mons Veneris, which is nothing else but an assembly or gathering together of Nymphs made in some certain den or cave of their world, not indeed in their Chaos but in the Chaos of men, but in the meantime in their Regions. The family of this Mons Veneris is very ancient of many years standing. They are long lived, without any defect in nature that is notable; they retain the same species always to the end of their life. But, now, Venus is both a Nymph and a Wave or Undine more worthy and superior than the rest, who hath reigned indeed a long time, but at length life is defunct. Whom another Venus hath succeeded but not like the former, to whom was given the government of domestical affairs, but she is dead at length, as also her kingdom. But as to the

Immortality of Venus, Philosophers differ, for some are of the opinion that she is the possessor of eternal life even to the day of Judgment. But, understand this of her and her seed, to wit, according to the species, not according to the Individuum. For the Last day will end and terminate all. Everything hath his end, they and all others die, but in the meantime in respect of seed, all generations continue till the last day.

The original of this Mons Veneris is thus recorded:— There was once a Nymph, some say a Queen, who lived on a mountain. This Nymph took occasion to leave that place and descended to a Lake in that Region, and there she built herself an habitation for love's zeal, which was defended by the mountain and without the doors a ditch, that a freer passage might be for her suitors and lovers.

Read the famous history of the Nymph that married Stauffenberg, whom some Divines will not allow otherwise than a diabolical delusion and not real, but it was true. She was an Undine, so called, and was married to one Stauffenberg and cohabited with him so long till he married another wife in regard he reckoned her for a Divorce, and that was the cause why he married another. But at the day of marriage, he sitting at the table, she appeared and gave him a sign of his breach of faith to her by striking him on the thigh, at the table, he being astonished therewith, the third day after he was found dead. This was a just punishment for adultery.

But to say something of Melusina, who was a Nymph who possessed a Sorceress. Such is Beelzebub's nature to transform such into other forms, as cats, or wolves, dogs, etc. Besides this she was a Nymph having flesh and blood, fruitful, disposed to generation, from the Nymphs she came out of the Earth to men to ensnare them, where she lived to the end of her life, how long that was God knows. This was a great fraud and treachery of Beelzebub. Superstition caused men to use Incantations to penetrate such places where such creatures were which remained with them like a Worm or Dragon of this kind to the end of their life.

Besides these, two more generations belong to the Nymphs and Pigmies. These are the generations of the Giants and Dwarves not descending from Adam. We must not refer St. Christopher to this class, because he was born of man's seed, but you must consult histories which give you account of Bernensis, Sigenot, Hildebrand Deitric and others, the like which were famous giants, as Laurinus was a famous dwarf. These giants were generated of the Sylphs, and the dwarfs came from the Pigmies, and of these are monsters or the Syrens of the Nymphs. The strength of these is wonderful as well as their appearance, which is rare. They exceed their own kind, the consideration of their prodigious acts and wicked designs. They are born of animals which are men, hence it follows that they have not their soul from their parents and being monsters, it consequently follows that they have no soul although they have become famous by many generous though abhorred crimes, as parrots know how to speak and Apes know how to act Man's gestures, so these by Nature's indulgence can express Man's deeds, but yet we cannot consider that they have a Soul. God can if he will infuse a Soul into these men like others, as the league between God and Man teaches, as well as the league of the Nymphs with Man, but they were born not for the Soul but for the Creature, that God might be seen therein more to be admired in his works. Neither would he create gigantic Souls, although one man may be like another in the Kingdom of God. Therefore, I compare them with animals whose soul is unknown to me; for although they shall do good and just things, I cannot say they are partakers of redemption, for they are not wise in faith, but lived like prudent animals. And if a wolf or fox could speak, they would not be much unlike them as to their intellect which is natural that so ready a judgment may be given of their soul.

Sylvestres or aerial men beget Giants, when they do meet in Conjunction, no otherwise than if a Conjunction should happen to a Comet, to an Earthquake and the like. But if it were requisite, a Monster should be born. According to the usual course of nature he is not born, but overthwart or crosswise according to the providence of God. But the Sylphs after their own way do copulate and bring forth monsters. Of the manner of which they are generated, nothing can be defined. For that work the order is Divine, nor otherwise can it be explained by Astronomy, of the wandering stars and of their generation, who have no rule after a natural manner, and are begotten and made, or the earthquake, which sometimes falls out and for a long time intermits. The like we must judge of the Giants who are born after the same manner by constellations of the same kind not indeed in heaven but as the constellations are made in Man. For the same heaven hath no force or operation to produce such monsters: with men, as to the constellation, with heaven there is no commerce. Indeed, all are under heaven and included of the same. But because it is another body, they have another Chaos, therefore, heaven can make no impression on them, because it sticks not nor lasts not. But here is to be understood a natural course and motion from the heaven as of these made by itself East and West. But here you must know that if any man be born more tall or more short, it must not be imputed to heaven, but to a peculiar course of nature. But of this I will be silent. Understand the like of the Dwarves which are born of the Pigmies of the earth, from whence they become not so tall, but in proportion are so much shorter by so much as the pigmies are more short than the Sylphs, these are no less monsters than the Giants and have the same manner of generation.

Consider what St. John the Baptist said to the Jews—God is able of these stones to raise up children unto Abraham. If it were possible to God to produce children from Adam's loins, the same God could make other men without his loins, as Nymphs, Giants, etc. Whereby he might as well increase as preserve his world. This may serve for our example and instruction, that God being powerful in one thing he is powerful in the other thing. If he can produce men seven feet long, he can also produce men that are 20 or 30 feet long. We see the example in Giants of whom we may learn that God is this Lord who is able to do all these things, and infuse a soul in a moment.

But to draw to a conclusion we must add that men of this kind, whether Giants or Dwarves, are fit to get with child women sprung from Adam, as to nature if like with like may square. But although these monsters are not fruitful, they are monsters only in their person, as to strength and magnitude not to generation, but as much as in them is beyond one seed they cannot evacuate; that is to say they attain not to the third and fourth generation. Furthermore, if they come to the generations of men, a double foetus or birth is begotten; that is to say, if it is bodied according to the nature of his mother then it requires her genius, otherwise it is generated like its animal the parent. But that there be made a mixture, which cannot be, for then the seed would have a greater force in the other. But although otherwise the two seeds may become one, but this is not in the like manner. And although there may be made one seed, it is qualified or separated from the other part which confers the soul. Therefore, after this manner their generations end, neither are heirs left to them. And as comets leave no children, and as an earthquake leave no seed after them, but together are ended as one in themselves. So they also in a degree or generation rise together and set.

Of the Cause of These Creatures

God in his infinite wisdom, set over keepers or preservers to all things in the universe, neither left he any thing unpreserved or without a keeper. So the Gnomes, Pigmies and Manes keep the treasures of the earth, that is to say, the metals and other things. From where they are conversant, there do lie hid great treasures and opulence. But there is a time defined when these treasures may be obtained, and we must beware that they be not brought to light before, which if men do find, they are wont to say in old time the Pigmies walked here, they are already gone, that is to say, the time was, that riches were proffered. From the treasures of the Earth are so distributed, that even from the beginning of the world, there are daily found metals, silver, gold, iron, etc., which are so kept from those men, that all everywhere go not forth in one day, but one by one. So the riches of the Mountains fly about, to and fro, according to time and regions being distributed from the first day to the last.

In like manner we must judge of the Salamanders, that they are the keepers of the fiery regions, wherein they are conversant. For in those regions are coined and fabricated those things which the Pigmies keep. For if the fire burns the Pigmies, then begin to watch, after whose watching the things are produced. After the same manner even the Sylphs keep the exterior gems which lie under the air, and fabricated of the Salamanders, and reserved in a due place where men may possess them. These jewels they defend, that they cannot be got till an appointed time. For where the like treasures lie, there these little men have their abode, taking care that these hidden riches shall not be enjoyed before a fit time, and have a right thereto. Therefore, since these men are the keepers of the goods of this kind, it may easily be understood that they indeed want a soul, but yet they are like unto men.

The Undines or Nymphs act in the waters and do keep these riches which are in the seas, and left and fabricated of the Salamanders. Therefore, in general we must note this of them, that wheresoever they are found, great treasures and the best of metals lie hid, of which they are ordained keepers.

Furthermore, such is the case and condition of the Syrens, Giants and Manes, as of the Scintillas or Sparks, which are only the monsters of the Salamanders, that indeed, they keep nothing but show some novelty or grand thing to men. So when any belchings of fire appears, a destruction is denounced to that country, for the most part a laying waste of that monarchy is presaged. In like manner, the Giants do portend great ruin and mischief will happen to that region. But the Manes or Ghosts of the dead, for the most part foretell to the people great want and poverty.

The Syrens do threaten sects and divisions and the destruction of Kings and Princes.

The main cause is hidden from us why and how these things are acted, but when the end of the world shall approach all these things from the least to the greatest shall be manifested, what manner of things they were, why and how they shall stand or walk and what they shall portend, for whatsoever thing was done in the whole world shall in that day be laid open. Every man shall then receive his reward according to his desert, then the darnel shall be separated from the wheat and the chaff from the corn.

Of Presaging

There are five manners of presaging or foretelling of events.

As to the first, the Prophets, Sybils and Disciples of Christ, foretold nothing by art but from the mouth of God.

The second kind of presaging came from nature itself, which showeth what good or bad anyone should make.

The third way of presaging is called Divination, whereby a man from his own light may foresee what end shall befall one.

The fourth way of presaging is by the help of Spirits, and this is called Sorcery.

The fifth kind of presaging is called Augury—to presage from the singing of birds, from the entrails of animals, from the inundations of waters, and from the violence of winds.

But the fourth way of presaging which is sorcery and contained under these four heads—Geomancy, Astromancy, Pyromancy and Hydromancy—which succeeds as Spirits do favour. This is the main subject of the Tabula Sancta, and I will particularly make a large discourse hereon. But now to put the Tables into practice, I will lay down Dr. Rudd's directions to know good Spirits from bad with the Invocations to visible appearance through all the Nine Hierarchies.

DR. RUDD'S
NINE HYERARCHES
OF ANGELS
WITH THEIR
INVOCATIONS
TO VISIBLE
APPEARANCE

scriptum per Pet. Smart A: M. Londiniensem
July 9th 1712

The Directory

The Signs

The Signs and Appearance both of good and evil Spirits are and ought to be carefully and well observed by reason they are foregoers of such appearances, and whereby are known the differences thereof which is a matter of material consequence as shall be more plainly showed forth.

Good Angels moved

If good Angels or Elemental powers of light or otherwise dignified Spirits of benevolent or symbolising nature with celestial powers, and allied to the welfare and preservation of mankind, are moved and called forth to visible appearance in a Crystal Stone or Glass Receiver as one usual way or customary form is among the learned Magicians, then the sign of their appearance most seemeth like a veil or curtain or some beautiful colour hanging in and about the stone or glass as a bright cloud or other pretty kind of Hieroglyphical show, both strange and very delightful to behold.

It is therefore to be remembered that the Magical Sophy ought to have for his purpose a Crystal Stone of a round globic form, very clear and transparent, or other stone of like diaphanity or ball of clear and solid glass or thick hollow glass with a little hole on the top of like form, of any convenient bigness or diameter according as can reasonably be obtained or made, and the same to be set in a frame, and also the Glass to be made with a stalk or shank fitted thereto and so to be put into a socket with a foot or pedestal to stand upright. The stone being called by the name of a Show Stone, and the Glass by the name of a Glass Receptacle, and in practice or action upon Invocation or motion made for spiritual appearance. There shall either be a wax candle on each side thereof, or a Lamp behind the same burning during the time of action set on a table apart fitted and furnished for the purpose. But if appearance hereof aforesaid be moved for, by Invocation out of the Show Stone or Glass Receptacle, or if yet notwithstanding appearance happen to show themselves out of them, yet the sign of their appearance will be very delectable and pleasant though various and amusing the senses to behold as a shining brightness, or sudden flashes or such like similitudes very splendid in show all about or in the place where action is made or appearance moved.

Invocation

When Invocation is made to any of the Celestial powers or dignified Elemental Spirits of light and appearance according is presented and visibly showeth itself either in the Show Stone or Glass Receptacle, or otherwise out of them, then view the same very well and also take notice of its corporature, physiognomy or features of the face, vestures or garments, deportment or behaviour, language or whatsoever else may be worthy of note by reason of making a fine distinction between the appearance of good angels or spirits, and others that are evil. And of knowing the same without being deceived; for although evil powers or spirits of darkness may be invocated, moved or called forth to visible appearance, and consulted withal and made use of in such concerns or upon such actions, wherein by nature and office they may be commanded to serve in all such matters, according as thereupon are dependent and as the necessities thereof shall be suitable and requisite. But then Actions with them are different both in time, place and order, and also the manner of operation which by them are diversely and severally elsewhere, hereafter inserted and showed forth in its proper place. Therefore do the Magick philosophers give this caution, saying—Beware that one Action, operation or secret in this Art be not mixed with another.

Action Apart

But let all Celestial, Elemental and Infernal actions, operations and Invocations be used and kept apart or separate, according to the method and manner, as are in particular ascribed and properly referred unto each of them. Now, then, observe that the appearance of Celestial and benevolent Angels and other dignified Elemental spirits or powers of light are to be thus known or distinguished from those that are infernal or evil powers or spirits of darkness. The good Angels or dignified powers of light as aforesaid, are in countenance very fair, beautiful, affable and youthful, smiling, amiable and usually of flaxenish or gold coloured hair, and in behaviour or gesture very courteous and friendly, in speech very gentle, mild, grave, eloquent, using no vain, idle or superfluous language or discourse. In their corporature very handsome, straight, comely, well favoured and in every limb most exactly formal and well composed; their motions sometimes to be plainly perceived, sometimes swift and sometimes imperceptible, both in their appearance, continuance and departure; and their garments and vestures of what fashion, form or colour soever thereof, are likewise very fair and beautiful or orient, and if it be of many colours or strange fashion, yet they are also very splendid, rare and lovely to behold, and in short, they are Celestially glorified in all their appearances, as they are in countenance and corporature most commonly beautiful, amiable and well composed without any of the least deformity either of hairiness in the face or body, or a swarthy complexion or any crookedness or either any ill shaped member of the body, so also are their garments or vestures without spot or blemish, either of being ragged or torn or stained or anywise to be seemingly dirty or daubed with any filthy, greasy or nasty soil, and always embrace the word Mercy.

Appearance

When the appearance of any Celestial Angels or Angelic powers of light or dignified Elemental Spirits are visibly showed forth and by good testimony or diligent observation well known to be so, then with due reverence given, thereto may be said as followeth.

Receive thus

Welcome be the light of the highest, and welcome be the Messengers of Divine Grace and Mercy, unto us, the true Servants and Worshippers of the same your God, whose Name be Glorified both now and for ever. Amen.

Good or Evil

And if the Appearance be of good, then it will stay, but if not it will immediately vanish or flow hastily away at the rehearsal of the word Mercy. But if any evil power shall appear in the place or stead of that which is good, and impudently withstand any opposition, then vanquish it as in this case. Evil spirits are to be dealt withal, in manner and form as hereafter is inserted in its place.

By reason these powers or spirits who are by nature evil and so are contrary to those by nature good, may not be dealt withal in those actions or operations. Nor those powers of light by nature good, to be moved in reference to what otherwise properly appertaineth or belongeth by nature and office to the evil powers or spirits of darkness, more than as for their assistance and so accordingly for deliverance from any violent surprises, assaults or illusions or other infernal temptations or envious attempts.

Expected Appearance

Now then, if by these Directions the expected Appearance is understood and found to be Celestial and of good, or to be dignified Elemental Spirits or powers of light and so likewise of good, as accordingly was Invocated, moved, or called forth to visible appearance, say thus—

Demand

Are ye the same whom we have moved and called forth to visible appearance here before us at this time by the name N or what else are ye and of what Order amongst blessed Angels or otherwise known or called by any mortal man, if you be of Celestial or Elemental verity and so of Charity, you cannot mislike or deny these our sayings.

Answer

Then if it maketh any Answer as peradventure it will, then make Reply according as the nature of your discourse requireth, but if it make no answer, then repeat the words aforesaid—Are ye the same, etc.

Then it will show forth or tell its name or office, the which when it is known by hearing, then it will speak or otherwise show forth. Say then as followeth.

Who it is

If you be **N** as you say, in the name of Jesus say, that all wicked Angels are justly condemned, and that by the mercy of God in the merits of Christ, Mankind Elect is to be saved.

Answer made, or be gone

Whereunto it will then return a satisfactory Answer or else it will depart or be gone away. Then if the Appearance be good (as may be known by the Answer) and the Reasons thereof that was made or given to the aforesaid proposition. Say as followeth.

Speak to the Appearance

O ye Servants or Messengers of Divine Grace or Mercy, and Celestial Angels or Angelic powers of light or dignified Elemental Spirits and Mediums of benevolence to Mankind, Servants of God. You, both now at this time and always, are and shall be unto us truly and sincerely welcome. Humbly desiring you to be friendly unto us, and to do for us in whatsoever it shall please God, to give by your Order and office to us for the better knowledge and benefit of mankind living on Earth, and make us partakers of true science and sapience in the undefiled and secret wisdom of your creation.

Answer Made

And if any Answer shall be made hereunto or any discourse from hence should arise or proceed hereupon, then both wisdom and reason must be the principal conduct in the managing thereof. But if there be silence and that no discourse arise from hence, then begin to make humble Request for Answer to such desires and proposals as in a certain writing is contained which ought to be in readiness with you, and then will the efforts of all things be undoubtedly and with good success determined.

Intrusion

The signs of Intrusion or appearance of evil when action or Invocation is otherwise made for moving or calling forth Celestial Angels or Intelligences or their dignified powers or Elemental spirits of light, are not apparent or visible to be any ways discernable more than the shapes, forms, gestures, and other like principles in appearance quite contrary in behaviour, language, clothing or vestures to those above related and to be observed of the good Angels. Neither are they herein otherwise to be judged of them, than as Intruders, Tempters and Illuders on purpose if possible to deceive and also destroy the perseverance and hopes of obtaining any benefit by Celestial and good Mediums, by reason that they are degraded and deprived of power to send or show forth any foregoing signs of their Appearance. In these are such superior actions Invocating or moving only Celestial or dignified Elemental powers and to visible appearances herein no ways to have further notice than to be vanquished and sent away, as before hath been said.

Observe then that the Corporature, forms and shapes of evil powers or spirits of darkness in their appearance by forcible Intrusions of this kind are easily to be discovered from the good powers and spirits of light as now shall be declared as followeth.

Of Evil Powers

Evil Powers or spirits of Darkness are ugly, ill favoured and beastly in shape and appearance, wherein observe if they appear in upright or human stature, then either body, face or covering are quite contrary to the other before specified of good. For although an Evil or Infernal Spirit may appear in the likeness of an Angel of light, especially in the time and place when good Angels or Spirits of light are Invocated, moved or called forth forming themselves very nearly, so even almost unperceived to the sight and apprehension except ingeniously discovered by curious observation and clearly may be discerned quickly by their raggedness, uncleanness of their garments and differences of their countenance in beauty and features and other decent composures of body, language and behaviour, and the corporeal difference of the limbs or bestial similitudes who in times do usually and suddenly make their appearance, and as readily show forth strange motions, gestures and speakings, unusual, blasphemous, ridiculous or different languages, altogether dissonant and contrary and very unlike both in matter and manner to that of the Celestial Angels and Elemental powers and other dignified spirits of light, which also may be soon discovered by the diligence of a sober and curious speculator. Which notable Intrusions they make on this action properly to destroy and if possible overthrow the reason, hope and Judgment of the Invocation, and by great errors, and other ignorant mistakes not only to deceive and confound the more solid and genuine knowledge and capacity of man labouring herein, but also to distract the senses, and thereby lead the understanding into a meander and therein to weary and tire us with verity of doubt, and desperation not knowing how to unravel this Gordian Knot or to be satisfied or delivered from the hopeless pilgrimage, but by the hope of Icarian wings.

From hence it may be understood that evil powers and spirits of darkness sooner appear as impudent Intruders in the time of good action, and in place where Invocation is made, for the moving and calling forth of any Good Angels or dignified Elemental powers or spirits of light to visible appearance, than at any other time or place. When as unto themselves they shall be indifferently by order, office and name Invocated, moved and called forth to visible appearance, for such is their assistance, as by nature and office wherein they are accordingly serviceable and suitable to the occasion wherein they were commanded. Therefore, in such actions, methods, form or observations as are to be only referred unto these evil powers or spirits of darkness. These actions we say are differently set apart and to be distinguished both in time, place, order and method, form and observation aforesaid, and so they may be moved and called forth, commanded and constrained, and accordingly so dealt withal and used as the present action shall require, and the discretion of the Invocant shall find agreeable to their nature and office. So then here it is observable, the Evil spirits may be invocated and dealt with differently and apart by themselves accordingly as aforesaid, but not in such place or at such time as when action or motion is made for the appearance of any Celestial or other dignified powers or Spirits of light and other Elemental powers or different spirits by nature good as well as evil and other wandering spirits non-resident in orders certain of like nature, etc., may be constrained and commanded by invocation to service and obedience, comparatively as vile slaves, accordingly as elsewhere in a particular treatise and Invocation properly thereto referred with several appurtenant rules and observations inserted therein as amply and at large showed forth. But Celestial Angels and other dignified Elemental powers and spirits of light by nature and office wholly benevolent and good, may not be commanded nor constrained by any Invocation. They are only to be moved and called forth by humble entreaties thereby acquiring favour and friendship.

When Wicked Intruders

Now then, if at any time or place where actions or motion are made, and humbly entreated, earnestly besought for the appearance of any Celestial Angel or dignified Elemental power or other spirit of light, and wicked Intruders shall impudently insinuate and thrust themselves in place and would enforce credulity into the Speculator. And that it shall be plainly discovered, then shall the Magical Sophy dismiss, discharge and send away and banish them from hence after this manner.

To Banish the Evil Spirits

The Vengeance of God is a two-edged sword cutting rebellious and wicked spirits of darkness and all other usurping powers in pieces. The hand of God is like a strong Oak, which when it falleth it breaketh in pieces many shrubs. The light of his eye expelleth darkness, and the sweetness of his mouth keepeth from corruption.

Blessed are all those to whom he showeth mercy and preserveth from temptation, and illusion of wicked Intruders, defending them by his mighty power under the Covert of Divine Grace, notwithstanding his humble servants to be overcome or overthrown by any infernal assaults. Now, therefore, because you have come hither and entered without license, seeking to entrap and ensnare us, and secretly conspired by these your subtilties to deceive and destroy us and our hopes, in the true meaning of these our sober, innocent, honourable and Celestial Actions and operations. We do in the great and mighty name and by the power of the most High God, triumph imperially over you, and by the virtue, force and efficacy thereof, be you and your powers vanquished, overthrown and utterly defaced and behold by virtue of that Celestial power by divine grace given to us and wherewith we are potently dignified, and as heirs of God's promise through faith continuing inherent in us. We do hereby wholly deface and overthrow you and ye are totally vanquished. Therefore, we say, depart and immediately be gone from hence in peace, without noise, turbulence, injury, harm, violence or other damage whatsoever. And as you are of darkness and the places of darkness, and have without any charge or permission enviously intruded, seeking thereby to ensnare, deceive and overwhelm us. The Divine Judgement and vengeance of the Most High God for this your wicked and malicious conspiracy and insinuation be your deserved reward, and as it was delivered to you, so take it with you, that the malice that you have shown us may heap up your own destruction. Be ye, therefore, dismissed and immediately we say, Depart hence unto your Orders and there to continue in the bonds of Confinement during the divine pleasure of the Highest.

If they are yet obstinate and impudent and will not depart, but rather will withstand the commands of the Magician, let him say as followeth.

To Vanquish

Do you thus impudently withstand and obstinately refuse to depart from our presence and from this place, and perniciously attempt yet further against us. IN THE NAME OF JESUS we say, Depart ye wicked seducers, and be ye immediately gone away from hence, and be it unto you according to the word of God, which judgeth righteously from evil unto worse, from worse unto confusion, from confusion to desperation, from desperation unto damnation, from damnation unto eternal death. Depart, therefore, we say unto the last Cry, and remain with the Prince of Darkness in punishment justly due as a fit reward unto your wicked malicious deservings. And the God of Mercy, graciously deliver us from you. Jehovah. Jehovah, Schah.

And if no Celestial Angels or other dignified spirits of light appear in place to vanquish and send away or seal up any wicked or

Infernal Spirits or spirits of darkness when Appearance is present as notorious Intruders in the time and place when Celestial or Elemental Actions with dignified powers of Light are in agitation and operation.

Rules to be Observed

Then let the discreet Magician with prudent passion have diligent regard to himself and consult the foregoing Rules according to respective and serious observation. Who then by the Office of himself will undoubtedly not only contract the sight and friendship of the Celestial Angels and also dignified Elemental and other benevolent spirits of light, to his relief and comfort, and to vanquish and overcome all evil spirits or powers of darkness. But also he shall have power to command, call forth and constrain all sublunary spirits and powers of all natures, orders and offices, both good and evil, light and darkness, or otherwise relating thereunto and bring them to such obedience, as according to their several and respective natures and office they may be so commanded and constrained to serve and obey.

A Second Introduction

When Invocation and Replication thereunto is amply made according to time, method, and order, and the Celestial Angel or Intelligence thereby moved doth appear, or any other Angel or Intelligence of the same Hierarchy, then mark and observe well the manner, shape, form, corporature, gesture, vestments and foregoing sign thereof, and if in all symbolical likelihood and probable symptoms the Apparition seemeth to be no less, or otherwise conjectured than what is from hence to be expected. Although that very Intelligence that was moved and called forth by name doth not appear, by reason it is of the superior order of the Hierarchy who are not always sent nor usually go forth neither are moved to visible appearance, but if especial grace and divine pleasure more especially unto choice and peculiar vessels of honour accordingly appointed immediately by the Holy Ghost to fulfil the Commands of the Highest, but yet some one or other or more of the Celestial powers of the same order as aforesaid, more inferior in degree, may be moved hereby to descend and appear at the earnest request of the Sophic Invocant, and perform whatsoever shall be requested according to its nature and office.

It cannot be unknown to any discreet Magician, that whensoever any good Angel or Celestial Intelligence is moved or called forth to visible experience, but also that evil spirits and infernal powers of darkness are immediately ready to encroach and appear in the room instead of the good Angels. Therefore, it behoveth to be very careful and greatly observing thereof, both the method and manner how to know and rightly to distinguish the appearance of the good angels or spirits from those that are evil, and how to deal with either of them. That is to say, how to receive good angels in their appearance and how to vanquish and banish Evil Spirits when they intrude and enter into place and presence, to deceive and overwhelm us. We have sufficiently and at large inserted and shown forth in our Directory, therefore, we shall in this place only show forth a method of our greeting the Apparition of any Celestial Angel or dignified power of light, and when by all the prescribed rules given, that apparition is truly known to be Celestial and of good, then humbly receive it with ample benevolence, saying as followeth.

To Receive a good Appearance

Welcome to the light of the Highest, and welcome to the Messengers of Divine Grace and mercy unto us, the true servants and worshippers of the same your God, whose name be glorified both now and for evermore.

When known to be Good

If the Appearance is perfectly known and understood, and by all the signs and tokens perfectly known to be Celestial or Angelical powers of light, then with due reverent observance say as followeth.

Receiving Good Angels

O you Servants or Messengers of divine grace and mercy and Celestial Angels, or Intelligences, powers of light, or dignified Elemental Spirits and Mediums of benevolence to mankind, Servants of God, you, both now at this time and always, are and shall be unto us truly and sincerely welcome. Humbly desiring you also to be friendly and do for us in whatsoever it shall please God to give by your Order and Office unto you for the better knowledge and benefit of mankind living here upon Earth, and to make us partakers of true sapience and science in the undefiled and sincere sacred wisdom of your Creation.

Answer

And if any Answer shall be made thereunto, or any discourses from hence should arise or proceed thereupon, then both wisdom and reason must be the principal conduct in the management thereof, but if there be silence that no discourse ariseth from hence, then begin to make humble request for answer to your desires and proposals, then will the effects of all things undoubted and with good success be determined.

Fear or Mistrust

But if there should any fear, doubt or just cause of jealousy be had or made of any expected apparition of any Angel or Intelligence of the Celestial Orders or other Elemental power of light, celestially dignified or otherwise, if at any time there should appear a spirit which you do think is not of good, or of the Order you moved for, or have any mistrust of it, the which you may easily perceive by form and also by its answering you in your question, then you may say to it as followeth.

To Know who it is

"In the name of JESUS who art thou?" Then perhaps it will say, "I am the Servant of God." Then you may say — "Art thou come from God? Art thou sent from him with good tidings or message?" Then perhaps it will say to you, or some such like words — "What I am he knoweth of whom I bear witness." Then you may ask its name, saying then — "What is your name? Either as it is notified among the blessed Angels or called by of mortal man, if you be of verity and so of charity you cannot mistake my speeches." Then it will tell you its name, or say nothing at all. But if it doth tell you his name, then you may say to it — "If you be in the name of Jesus, say that all wicked Angels are justly condemned, and that by the mercies of God in the merits of Christ, Mankind elect is to be saved." Then it will give you a sufficient answer to satisfy you or else it will be gone from you. And then if it be of good and hath answered your request, then perhaps it will say, "Thus much thou hast required." Then you may say — "I did so for so is his Judgement and Justice against the Impertinent and his mercy to his Elect. Test is Truth. "

Then you may ask your desire.

We thought good to instance thus much for better Information and Instruction, although a full narrative hereof is amply and at large showed forth in the foregoing Directions or Directory, both as to the knowing and receiving of good Angels or Celestial Intelligences or other Elemental Spirits or powers of light Angelically or

Celestially dignified, and for the knowledge vanquishing and driving away of all evil spirits and infernal powers of darkness whensoever any such Apostate shall forcibly intrude or make entrance or appearance instead of Celestial and good Angels or other dignified Elemental powers of light, in the time and place of these actions, purposively to deceive and confound and utterly if possible to destroy the hopes and expectations, comforts and benefits of the sophic Philosophers in their elaborate industry and care and earnest addresses unto the Celestial Angels and blessed Intelligences or dignified Elemental powers or other spiritual Mediums or Messengers of divine light for the true knowledge and finding out the true use of all physical and metaphysical arcanums or secrets in a superior or profound mystery, which cannot otherwise be known or found out but by the divine light and conduct of Angelical Ministry or other Spiritual Revelation and instruction by such mediums of benevolence to Mankind as through the divine grace, mercy and goodness of the highest as are by nature, order and office thereunto preordinately decreed and appointed.

But as touching the insisting any further of this matter we think it needless; since it is more full treated of in the foregoing Directory which we advise to be well understood by a due and serious consideration, before any progress or unadvised proceedings are made herein.

Observe, also, whereas we have severally and particularly mentioned Celestial Angels or blessed Intelligences and Elemental powers of light and other dignified spirits of light who are by nature and office good and also friendly and benevolent unto mankind, and generally inserted them together with material distinction, yet let the grave and sober Magicians take notice that consideration be first had, of what Angel or Intelligence, of what spirit, or of what order and office, he would move or call forth and so in particular to make mention thereof accordingly and not otherwise, whereunto everything ought by order, nature, degree and office, properly to be referred.

Here endeth the Isagogical Preface
or Second Introduction

A PRAYER TO BE SAID
before the Moving or Calling Forth
Any of the Celestial Intelligences
to Visible Appearance
by the Following
KEYS OR PROVOCATIONS

O Almighty Immortal Immense Incomprehensible and Most High God, the only Creator of Heaven and Earth, who by thy Word alone hast in they Omniscience among the rest of thy marvellous and wonderful works placed and appointed many Hierarchies of sacred Celestial Angels from thy mighty and unspeakable Throne unto the fiery Region as ministering spirits of several names, natures, degrees, Orders, and offices, residing in those Eleven Orbs or Spheres placed one above the other as the proper Mansions of those blessed Angels or Mediums or superior Messengers, both mediate and immediate of divine grace, light and mercy, and amongst the sons of men from the beginning of time called sacred Celestial Intelligences from the Orb, Region Element of fire, from the superior to the inferior in their several and respective Orbicular Mansions, Orders and Offices, do serve before thee and obey thy Commandments and most high Commands as in thy divine will and pleasure in the unity of the blessed Trinity is decreed and appointed, and also by thy most gracious and merciful permission to minister unto and illuminate the understanding of thy servants, the sons of men, and by their frequent appearance verbal converse, friendly community, Angelic Archidoctions and other spiritual Instincts continually, from time to time and at all times directing, instructing and inspiring them in all true science and sapience, and also to fulfil thy divine will and good pleasure therein to all such of thy humble and true servants whom thou art graciously pleased to show forth thy bountiful and paternal mercies.

We thy most sinful and undutiful Servants, unworthy of the least of thy blessings, yet with an assured confidence of thy heavenly benignities, do in thy holy fear, humbly prostrate our-

selves before thy Almighty presence, at the sacred feet of thy
fatherly goodness and clemency in all contrition of heart and
earnestness of spirit, humbly beseeching thy Omnipotent Majesty
to have mercy, pity and compassion upon us, and to pardon all our
sins and offences that we have committed against thee, and in thy
infinite mercy graciously to dignify us with celestial dignity by the
power of thy holy spirit and grant that these, thy glorious ministering Angels or blessed Intelligences, who are said to govern or reside
in the nine Orbs, orders or Hierarchies, as they are severally and
respectively therein placed and set over.

That is to say:
   1 METHRATTON in the ninth moveable Heaven in the Order
of Seraphims,
   2 RAZIEL in the highest Orb or Starry Heaven or firmament in
the Order of Cherubims,
   3 CASSIEL or Zaphkiel and Jophiel in the seventh Orb or
Heaven of Saturn in the Order of Thrones,
   4 SACHIEL or Zadkiel in the sixth Orb or Heaven of Jupiter in
the Order of Dominations,
   5 SAMAEL in the fifth Orb or Heaven of Mars in the Order of
Potestates,
   6 MICHAEL and Uriel in the fourth Orb or Heaven of Sol in the
Order of Virtues,
   7 ANAEL in the third Orb or Heaven of Venus in the Order of
Principalities,
   8 RAPHAEL in the second Orb or Heaven of Mercury in the
Order of Archangels,
   9 GABRIEL in the first Orb of Heaven of Luna of the Order of
Angels,

messengers of Divine Grace from the Superior to the Inferior,
residing and bearing office in each respective Orb of Heaven and
Hierarchies severally and distinctly in general and particular, and
also all others thy benevolent Messengers, Spirits of light, and
residing in the Orbicular Spheres, Angels, Orders, Mansions, Divisions and the Heavens by thy divine goodness and permission, and

at our humble request, Invitations and Invocations, may move, descend and appear to us in this Crystal Stone or Glass, which we shall call receptacles as being convenient for the receiving of all Angelical and spiritual presence in their Appearances, and so for that purpose set here before us.

The which we beseech thee, Lord, to bless and to dignify, first with thy omnipotent Confirmation, and secondly by the Influence of the Angelical Confirmations by them conveyed, therefore, and conjoined thereunto, and also by their splendid presence in action and that in and through the same, they may transmit their luminous rays or true and real presence in appearance to the sight of our eyes and their voices to our ears, that we plainly and visibly see them and hear them speak unto us or otherwise to appear out of them or besides them visibly to be seen and to be heard of us, as shall please thy Divine will and shall best or most benefit and comfort and also befitting our convenience in these actions, Inquisitions, matters or things.

That we thus humbly beseech thee to give and grant unto us and all things else that shall be necessary for us, which great benefits thou hast been pleased mercifully heretofore to emit and give our ancestors and forefathers, and also lately to such of thy Servants (as we have humbly, faithfully, unfeignedly and obediently besought thee for true wisdom by Divine and Angelical Inspirations and Instruction), which they have fully enjoyed by the ministry of thy sacred Angels.

THE
NINE GREAT
COELESTIAL KEYS
OR
ANGELICAL INVOCATIONS

The Nine Great Celestial Keys
or Angelical Invocations

moving or calling forth to visible appearance the Governing Angels or blessed Intelligences and all other the Celestial ministering Angels and Mediums Spiritual of divine light, grace and virtue, locating residing and bearing rule in the Seven Orbs, heavenly Mansions or Spheres and properly referred to the seven planets, the starry firmament or First Mover who therein according to each and every of their several respective Hierarchies, Orders and Offices whereunto they distinctly appertain, do serve and obey the commands of the Most High God, and both immediately and mediately as Messengers and servants spiritual of Divine grace and light and mercy, fulfilling his omnipotent decrees, determinations and appointments as dispensable and disposed of at his omniscient will and pleasures, and who are frequently conversant and familiar with such holy pious and devout men living on Earth, wheresoever they are by them called forth to visible appearance as either may or fitly shall be qualified therefor, or otherwise endowed with Celestial gifts, blessings and confirmations by Angelical mystery or divine grace more superior.

KEY NAME	ANGEL	HIERARCHY OF ORB	NUMBER OF
First	Methratton	Seraphim	Ninth
Second	Raziel	Cherubim	Eighth
Third	Cassiel	Thrones	Seventh
Fourth	Sachiel	Dominations	Sixth
Fifth	Samael	Potestates	Fifth
Sixth	Michael	Virtues	Fourth
Seventh	Anael	Principalities	Third
Eighth	Raphael	Archangels	Second
Ninth	Gabriel	Angels	First

[The copyist of this manuscript chose to write out these Nine Conjurations as they would be spoken. However, the framework of each Conjuration is exactly the same, only the particular constellation of Angelic Name, Hierarchy, Heaven, Number of Orb, Sephirah, and Divine Name are changed with each Conjuration. I have chosen instead to print out the text once only and list the corresponding names and attributes to be inserted for each Angelic Conjuration. Although this may seem a rather clumsy method, I felt it unnecessary to print out nine separate versions of the one formula. Also, this forces those readers intending to use such conjurations to actively hold these correspondences in their consciousness and not merely read these conjurations and prayers off the printed page.—*Editor*]

HEAVEN	SEPHIRAH NAME	DIVINE
Prime Mover	Kether	Eheia
Fixed Stars	Hokmah	Iod Jehovah
Saturn	Binah	Tetragrammaton Elohim
Jupiter	Hesed	El
Mars	Geburah	Elohim Gibor
Sol	Tiphereth	Eloha
Venus	Nezach	Adonai Sabaoth
Mercury	Hod	Elohim Sabaoth
Luna	Hesod	Sadai Elhai

THE NINE KEYS

moving or calling forth to visible appearance the Celestial Hierarchies of Angels of the Order of [**Hierarchy**] whose principal governing Angel or blessed Intelligence bearing rule is [**Angel Name**] and residing in the [**Number of Orb**] Orb, Mansion or Sphere called the [**Heaven**].

THE PRAYER OR INVOCATION

O you great glorious, sacred and Celestial Angel or blessed Intelligence who is called [**Angel Name**] and all other the Celestial Angels, Servants of the Most High Omnipotent, Incomprehensible, Immense, Eternal God of Hosts, the only Creator of Heaven and Earth and of all things whatsoever, both Celestial, Elemental, Animal, Vegetable, Mineral, and Reptile or Insect, that is contained or comprehended therein and serving as ministering Angels present always before him at his most high superior and divine commands and appointments in the Order or Hierarchy of Angels called [**Hierarchy**] and residing in the [**Number of Orb**] Heaven and bearing office, rule and power in the Mansion, Orb or Sphere called the [**Heaven**].

We, the Servants also of the Highest, reverently here present in his holy fear, do call upon, humbly request, earnestly entreat and move you to visible appearance in, by and through this most excellent, ineffable, great, mighty, signal, sacred and divine name of the Most High God [**Divine Name**] and his numeral attribute [**Sephira**] who sitteth in the most Imperial and highest heaven, before whom all the Host or Choir of Celestial Angels incessantly sing O MAPPA-LA-MAN-HALLELUJAH, and by the Seal of your Creation being the mark of Character of Holiness unto you, and by the occult mystery, secret virtue, efficacy and influence thereof dignifying and confirming you in orders, office, name, nature and corporeality with Divine, Celestial, Angelical, Immortal, Eternal, and sublime excellency, glory, power, purity, perfection, goodness and love, first unto the service of the most High God, and his Divine Laws and Commands and next unto the charge, care, conduct, counsel, comfort, benefit and assistance of his servants the Sons of men living on Earth to inspire, instruct and guide them into the knowledge and way of truth, and all true physical and Metaphysical Sciences, either immediately from the Holy Ghost unto more choice vessels of honour or mediately by Divine Grace and permission from yourself or selves unto the sons of men, servants of God dwelling upon Earth, whensoever you shall be of them Invocated and called forth and thereby moved to descend and appear unto them, and by all aforesaid, and by the great signal virtue, power, dignity, excellency and efficacy thereof, both immediately primary and mediately secondary be respective Mediums of divine light, grace and mercy as ordinately dependant, and so thereby flowing and accordingly diffusing by several emanations proper as symbolizing power and virtue from the Superior to the Inferior.

We do humbly beseech, earnestly request and incessantly entreat you, O you magnific, benevolent and sacred Angel or blessed Intelligence [**Angel Name**] who is said to be the principal Celestial Angel or blessed intelligence governing in the [**Number of Orb**] Heaven, Orb or Sphere called [**Heaven**] together with all others, the benevolent sacred and Celestial Angels or Intelligences, Ministers of truth and true science and sapience, both celestial and terrestrial, Messengers spiritual of light and Mediums of divine grace located, bearing rule, and residing in the Order and Hierarchy and Office called [**Hierarchy**] in the [**Number of Orb**] Heaven, Orb or Sphere of [**Heaven**] from the Superior to the Inferior, in general and particular, jointly and severally, every and each one by office and degree respectively, and to gird up and gather your selves together, and some one or more of you as it shall please God and by divine permission to move and descend from your Celestial mansion or place of residence into this Crystal Stone or Glass Receiver and therein to appear visibly unto us.

And we do also entreat you would be favourably pleased in and through the same to transmit your true Angelical and real presence plainly unto the sight of our eyes, and your voice unto our ears, that we may visibly see you and audibly hear you speak unto us, or otherwise to appear out of the same, as it shall please God and you his servants of divine grace and Messengers of mercy, seemeth most meet, proper, pertinent or best befitting this action, appearance, occasion or matter, and to show plainly and visibly unto us a foregoing sign or test of your appearance and we also yet further humbly beseech you, earnest entreat, undeniably request and move you, O you benevolent and glorious Angel and blessed Intelligence [**Angel Name**] together with all others, the sacred Celestial Angels or Intelligences from the Superior to the Inferior in power and Office, residing in the [**Number of Orb**] Orb or Sphere, called the [**Heaven**] Heaven, and serving the divine decrees, commands and appointments of the highest in the office and order of [**Hierarchy**] in, through and by this divine Signal Majesty and powerful Name of your God [**Divine Name**], Numeral Attribute [**Sephira**], and the great efficacy, virtue, excellency, power, prevalency and superiority thereof, to give up and gather your selves together every and each one jointly and by itself respectively and severally to move and descend from your Celestial Mansion or place of residence, apparently visible to the sight of our eyes in this Crystal Stone or Glass Receiver standing here before us as being set for this purpose, or otherwise unto us and before us out of the same, as it shall please God and you his servants of divine grace, light and mercy, seemeth best befitting this action, and also to show forth a preceding sign of your appearance and to be friendly unto us, and by your Angelical benevolence, Celestial Illumination, favourable assistance, familiar society, mutual correspondency, verbal converse, continual community and sacred instructions, both now at this time present and at all other times, to inform and rightly direct our more weak, depraved, stupid and ignorant Intellect, Judgment and understandings, and to conduct us by your Angelical Instincts and Archidoctions into the luminous pathway of truth, leading and giving entrance into the ports, cities and palaces of wisdom and true sapience, and to make us partakers of undefiled knowledge, without whose angelical guide, Spiritual Conduct, blessed assistance and benevolent advertisement, it is very difficult if not impossible for us or any mortal on Earth, to find or obtain or to be esteemed worthy of entrance into with testimony.

Wherefore, we humbly entreat and move you, O you great sacred and Celestial Ministering Angel or Intelligence [**Angel Name**] and all other the president and inferior Angels and Servants of the most High God residing and officiating in the [**Number of Orb**] Heaven, Mansion, Orb or Sphere of [**Heaven**] in the Order and Hierarchy of Angels called [**Hierarchy**] who all obediently serve and readily fulfil his omnipotent decrees and Commandments in his divine dispensations and appointments, according to your general and respective offices, in, by and through, this his ineffable Imperial great signal and divine name [**Divine Name**] and his Numeral Attribute [**Sephira**], and by the power, virtue and efficacy thereof, we the servants of the same your God and by the strength and force of our hope and faith in Him for divine assistance, grace and mercy, therein do earnestly request, powerfully invocate and confidently move you and call you forth to visible appearance here by us in this Crystal Stone or Glass Receiver, or otherwise thereat as it shall please God is given unto you so to do, and likewise to show visibly unto us a foregoing sign of your appearance.

O you Servant of mercy [**Angel Name**], and all other the Celestial ministering Angelic Messengers, Mediums of divine grace and light from the superior to the inferior, residing, serving and officiating in the Order of [**Hierarchy**] move, we say, and by superior power and permission in the name of the Highest, descend and appear and visibly show yourself, jointly and severally and respectively unto us in this Crystal Stone or Glass Receiver standing here before us or otherwise out of the same, as it shall please God to appoint and permit you, and to show us a preceding sign thereof. And by your immediate Angelical Inspiration and information and chief teaching to instruct, help, aid, and assist us, both now at this time present and also at other times and places whensoever and wheresoever we shall Invocate, move or call you forth to visible appearance and to our assistance in whatsoever truth and subject matter or thing appurtaining thereunto in all wisdom and true science, both Celestial and terrestrial and that shall be necessary for us and also as any other emergent occasion shall properly and duly require to the advancement and setting forth of God's glory and the improvement of our welfare and comfort, and benefit of our worldly and temporal estate and condition while we yet live, and likewise in all such matters or things whatsoever else that shall be necessary for us to know and enjoy, even beyond what we are able to ask or think, which the Almighty Giver of all good gifts shall in his bountiful and paternal Mercy be graciously pleased hereby to give you to reveal and show forth unto us or otherwise to bestow upon us.

O you great Angel or blessed Intelligence [**Angel Name**] and all other you Celestial Angels of the order of [**Hierarchy**] Mediums of divine grace and mercy, Ministers of true light and understanding and Servants of the most high God, particularly recited and respectively spoken of, Invocated, moved and called forth to visible appearance as aforesaid; Descend, we say, and by the power of superior commission from one or more of you, appear visibly here before us, as for the Servants of the most high God, whereunto we move you all, jointly and severally, in power and presence, whose works shall be a Song of honour and the praise of your God in your Creation. Amen.

Let the foregoing Invocation be devoutly and seriously read and uttered. Then make a pause for about 9 minutes of time, which is a little more than half a quarter of an hour, and if nothing yet appear within the Crystal Stone or Glass Receiver or otherwise out of them to visible appearance, then read with good devotion and serious Observance as aforesaid, this following Replication, three, four or five several times, observing the like pause or a little space of time aforesaid betwixt every each Replication.

REPLICATION

O, you glorious Angel or blessed Intelligence, who by name is called [**Angel Name**] and all other the sacred Celestial Angels of the Order of [**Hierarchy**], residing and located by Mansion proper in that Mansion, Orb or Sphere of Heaven called the [**Heaven**], [**Number of Orb**] Moveable Heaven, particularly recited, mentioned, moved and called forth to visible appearance as in the foregoing Invocation is and hath been of us lately and more at large rehearsed, humbly solicited, supplicated and earnestly requested, by the virtue, power, force and efficacy whereof and of all the Royal words and sentences therein contained, and also by the mighty, great, powerful and excellent name of the most high God [**Divine Name**] and his Numeral Attribute [**Sephira**] or otherwise by the truest and most especial name of your God.

We the servants also of the highest, reverently here present in his holy fear, attending his divine grace, mercy and good pleasure paternally unto us therein; Do by the strength and power of our faith, hope and confidence of and in our God and our Confirmation in his Holy Spirit, dignifying us with superior power and perfection, humbly entreat and earnestly request and powerfully move you, O you great Angel or blessed Intelligence, from the Superior to the Inferior, in general and in particular, every and each one, for and by itself, respectively by degree, nature and office, residing in the Mansion or [**Number of Orb**] or the [**Number of Orb**] Moveable Heaven, and serving the commands of the Highest in the Order and Hierarchy of Angels called [**Hierarchy**].

Move, therefore, O you great and glorious Angel [**Angel Name**] or some one or more or either of you, O ye sacred Celestial Angels of the Order of [**Hierarchy**] by degree, nature and office, and by the power, virtue and efficacy of all aforesaid, descend and appear visibly unto us in this Crystal Stone or Glass Receiver or otherwise out of the same here before us as it shall please God and also you his Celestial Messengers of divine grace and mercy and to show forth plainly unto us some remarkable sign or token foregoing your coming and appearance, and be friendly unto us and do for us as for the Servants of the Highest, whereunto in his name we do again earnestly request and move you both in power and presence, whose friendship unto us herein and works shall be a Song of honour and the praise of your God in your Creation.

THE SEAL OF METHRATTON
AND THE EXPLANATION

Eheia, the name of the Divine Essence. His Idea is called Kether, signifies a Crown or Diadem, hath his influence by the Order of Seraphim, or as the Hebrews call them Hayioth Hacadesch, i.e. Creatures of Holiness, and then by the Primum Mobile, whose particular Intelligence is called Methratton, that is the Prince of Faces, whose duty it is to bring others to the face of the Prince. And by him the Lord spake to Moses.

THE SEAL OF RAZIEL
AND THE EXPLANATION

Iod Tetragrammaton signifieth the Divinity full of Ideas. His numeral attribute Hochma, that is Wisdom, the first begotten, and is attributed to the Son and hath his influence by the Order of Cherubim, or that the Hebrews call Orphanim, that is forms or Wheels, and from thence into the starry firmament or Heaven where he fabricateth so many figures as he hath Ideas in himself, and distinguisheth the very Chaos of the Creatures by particular Intelligence called Raziel, who was the ruler of Adam.

THE SEAL OF CASSIEL
AND THE EXPLANATION

Tetragrammaton Elohim, his numeral attribute or Idea is Bina, viz., Providence and understanding attributed to the Holy Spirit, hath influence by the Order of Thrones, which the Hebrews call Great Angels or Aralim, mighty and strong, and from thence by the Sphere of Saturn administreth form to the unsettled matter, whose particular Intelligence is Zazel, or Zaphkiel the ruler of Noah, and another Intelligence named Iophiel, the Ruler of Sem, and these are three supreme and high Ideas, as it were seats of the Divine persons by whose commands all things are made but are executed by the other seven upon Earth, which are therefore called the Divine Ideas framing.

THE SEAL OF SACHIEL
AND THE EXPLANATION

El, the strong powerful Name of God, his Idea or numeral attribute Hesed which is Clemency or goodness, and signifieth Grace, mercy, piety, magnificence, the sceptre and the right hand, and hath his influence by the Order of Dominations, which the Hebrews call Hasmalim, and so through the Sphere of Jupiter, fashioning the Images of bodies bestowing Clemency and pacifying Justice on all. His particular Intelligence is Sachiel the ruler of Abraham.

THE SEAL OF SAMAEL
AND THE EXPLANATION

Elohim Gibor, i.e. the Mighty God punishing the wicked. His idea or numeral attribute is called Geburah, that is power, gravity, fortitude, security, Judgement, punishing by slaughter and war, and it is applied to the tribunal of God, the Girdle, the Sword, and the Left Hand of God, it is also called Pachai which is fear, and hath his influence through the order of Powers, which the Hebrews call Seraphim, and these through the sphere of Mars illuminate the Rosy Crucians, to whom belong fortitude and prudence. It draweth forth the Elements, and his particular Intelligence is Camael the ruler of Samson.

THE SEAL OF MICHAEL AND THE EXPLANATION

Eloha, Tree of Life is his Idea, Tiphereth his Sephiroth or numeral attribute, it signifieth apparel, beauty, glory, pleasure, hath his influence through the Order of Virtues, which the Hebrews call Malachim, that is Angels into the Sphere of the Sun giving brightness and life unto it, and from thence producing metals. His particular Intelligence is Michael, who was the ruler of Isaac, Raphael the ruler of Toby the Younger and the Angel Peliel ruler of Jacob.

Now for to receive this from the operation of the Sun, make an Image in the hour of the Sun, Leo then ascending and the Sun in it. The figure is a King crowned, sitting in a chair, having a Raven on his hand. It must be cast in Gold, and then the virtue is brought down by Verchiel, the spirit that instantly will rest upon it. This spirit is strong, fair coloured like a temperate and well proportioned man, choleric, having a voice barren. By this spirit, young Toby spake to Raphael and it aided him to fetch his father's Gold and also bound the evil spirit Asmodaeus.

THE SEAL OF ANAEL
AND THE EXPLANATION

Adonai Sabaoth or Tetragrammaton Sabaoth, that is the God of Hosts, and his Idea is Nezah, that is, Triumph and Victory. It signifieth the Eternity and Justice of a revenging God. He hath his influence through the Order of Principalities, whom the Hebrews call Elohim, that is the Lords into the Sphere of Venus, gives zeal and love of righteousness, and produceth vegetables. His Intelligence is Anael, and the Angel Cerviel, the ruler of David.

THE SEAL OF RAPHAEL
AND THE EXPLANATION

Elohim Sabaoth signifieth the God of Hosts, not of war and Justice for his name signifieth both, and precedeth his army. His numeral attribute Idea or Sephiroth is Hod which is interpreted both praise, confession, honour and famousness. It hath influence through the Order of the Archangels which the Hebrews call Ben Elohim, that is the Sons of God, into the sphere of Mercury and gives eligancy and constancy of speech and produceth living creatures. His Idea is Michael who was the ruler of Solomon. His Intelligence is Raphael, the ruler of Tobias. He giveth clemency, grace, mercy, piety, magnificence, eligancy, wisdom, virtue, industry, faith, religion, royalty, gravity of speech, honesty and acuteness of wit.

The ancient Magicians made an Image hollow or Telesme of Quicksilver, with the figure of a handsome young man bearded on it, then the Genius will speak with a barren voice yet very audible. Sometimes Derachiel, or Ambiel or Gabriel will descend upon the Telesme. These Genii are strong, fair coloured, with a human voice. These were the rulers of Solomon, are exceeding loving and will often stir you up to call the God that made all the World, and to pray to him and his son Jesus Christ that died on the Cross for our Redemption. These Genii help the memory, cure all distempers of the brain, Melancholy, they teach the causes of distempers of heat and cold, and finally teach all things you can name or think on.

THE SEAL OF GABRIEL
AND THE EXPLANATION

The Ninth Name of God falls upon the seventh planet. It is called Sadai, that is, Omnipotence, satisfying all, and Elhai, which is the living God. His numerical attribute or Sephiroth is Iesod, that is, Foundation, and signifieth a good understanding, a Covenant, Redemption and rest, and hath influence through the Order of Angels into the sphere of the Moon, causing the increase and decrease of all things, and taketh care of the Ideas of the Earth, of the Rules of the 12 divisions, and of their Images and Figures, and of the Genii or keepers of men and distributeth them. His Intelligence is Gabriel who was the keeper of Joseph, Joshua and Daniel.

In the hour of the Moon on a Monday, Magicians raise the first face of Cancer, the Moon in the Ascendant or in her Exaltation Taurus, the figure they then melted in Silver, was a man leaning on a staff, having a bird on his head and a flourishing tree before him; upon which descends the Angel Seheliel, and he causeth increase of gain, and is good against weariness. The second figure they made the Moon ascending in that part of Cancer, was a woman cornuted, riding on a bull. And in the third part they made a figure riding upon a Dragon with seven heads, or a Crab, and in her right hand a dart, in her left a looking glass clothed or covered with white or green and having on her head two serpents with horns twined together, and to each arm a serpent twined about, and at each foot also. And then they Invocated the Angel Muriel, which is the chiefest of the Deities, the first of the Goddesses, the Queen of Angels, the Mistress of the Elements whom the stars answer when the Moon with her seasons returns. Elements serve her, at whose nod the Lightnings breathe forth, seeds bud, plants increase, the initial parent of fruit.

She is the satellite of the Moon, restraining the various passions of the Stars, dispensing various lights by the circuits of the Sun: the Lady of great beauty, the Mistress of rain and water, the giver of Justice, the Nurse of mankind, the governor of all states; kind, merciful, protecting men by sea and land, mitigating all tempests of fortune, and dispensing with fate, nourishing all things growing on Earth, wandering and shining in the tops of high woods and groves, beholding the playing of Fairies, restraining the rage of Goblins, shutting the openings of earth and dispensing the light of the heaven, the wholesome rivers of the sea, the deplored silence of the infernal gods, by its motion ruling the world, and treading Hell under her feet; of whose Majesty the birds hasting in the air are afraid, the wild beasts straying in the mountains, serpents lie hid in the ground, fishes swimming in the sea. She cureth diseases phlegmatic, catarrhs, dropsy, gout and fluxes of the stomach for want of digestion.

HASMODAI or ☽ in ♋, in Geomancy Populus ruleth by day.

MURIEL by night or Via. (See my Explanation of Enoch's Tables).

```
  ★   ★
  ★   ★      Populus
  ★   ★
  ★   ★
```

```
       ★
       ★       Via
       ★
       ★
```

The Olympian Spirits

To conclude Dr. Rudd's Doctrine of the Nine Hierarchies of Angels and the better to understand him, that although the glorious Methratton and Raziel may be invoked for some great signal and weighty matters to prevent ruin of states and kingdoms and persons in great authority, yet it is the opinion of Dr. Dee and Dr. Rudd, and Iamblichus that ancient magician, that it is rarely practiced since the Olympic powers are sufficient to be invoked and advised with.

For there are seven different Governments of the spirits of Olympus, by whom God hath appointed the whole frame and Universe of this world to be governed and their visible stars are Saturn, Jupiter, Mars, the Sun, Venus, Mercury and the Moon.

Every Olympic Power rules 490 years.

In the beginning of their simplex Anomaly in the 60 years before the Nativity of Christ was the administration of Bethor, and it lasted until the year of Christ 430, to whom succeeded Phaleg until the 920th year. Then began Och and continued until the year 1410 and thenceforth Haggith ruleth until the year 1900.

THE FIRST OLYMPIC SPIRIT
SATURN — ARATRON

Saturn, who is called Aratron, ruleth visible provinces 49. He appeareth in the first hour on Saturday and very truly giveth answers concerning the provinces and provincials, and hath in his power, those things ascribed to the power of Saturn. His Seal is above — the Talitsman, Seal or Character. The Chaldaic word Tsilmonia comes from the Hebrew צלם Tselem, which signifies an Image and the Arabic word Talitsman signifies the same.

The Telesmatical Images of Saturn and Zazel, they are made for the most part with tall lean and slender bodies, with an angry countenance having four faces, one in the hinder part of the head, one on the forepart of the head, and on each side nosed or beaked. There likewise appeareth a face on each knee, of a black shining colour. Their motion is the moving of the winds, with a kind of Earthquake. Their sign is white earth, whiter than snow.

The forms peculiar to the Spirits of Saturn, they are called particular forms, they arise from Capricorn and Aquarius called by magicians, Cambiel and Anael, and their Geomantic Figures Tristitia and Carcer.

```
    *    *                          *
    *    *                      *    *
    *    *    Tristitia         *    *    Carcer
         *                         *
```

[viz. See Tabula Sancti Enochi.]

A King having a beard, riding on a Dragon
An old man with a beard
An old woman leaning on a staff
A hog
A Dragon
An owl
A black garment
A hook or sickle
A Juniper tree.

1   Aratron of his own free will can convert any thing into a Stone in a moment, either animal or plant, retaining the same object to the sight.
2   He converteth treasure into coals and coals into treasure.
3   He giveth familiars with a definite power.
4   He teacheth Alchymy, Magic and Physic.
5   He reconcileth the Subterranean spirits — maketh hairy men.
6   He causeth men to be invisible.
7   The barren he maketh fruitful and giveth long life and hath under him 49 Kings, 42 Princes, 35 Presidents, 28 Dukes, 21 Ministers standing before him, 14 familiars, 7 Messengers, and commandeth 36,000 Legions of spirits. Every Legion is 490.

THE SECOND OLYMPIC SPIRIT
JUPITER — BETHOR

Bethor ruleth visible provinces 32, governeth those things which are ascribed to Jupiter. He soon cometh being called. He that is dignified with his character he raiseth to very great dignities, to cast open treasures. He reconcileth the spirits of the air that they give true answers, they transport precious stones from place to place and they make medicines to work miraculously in their effects. He giveth also the familiars of the firmament and prolongeth life to 700 years if God's will. He hath under him 42 Kings, 35 Princes, 28 Dukes, 21 Councillors, 14 Ministers, 7 Messengers, and commandeth 29,000 Legions of spirits.

The Telesmes of Jupiter and Hismael

The Images of Jupiter they make with a body sanguine and choleric, of a middle stature with a horrible fearful motion but with a mild countenance; a gentle speech, and of the colour of Iron; the motion of them is flashings of lightning and thunder; their sign is, they say, there will appear men about the place where action is performed who should seem to be devoured of Lions.

Their particular or familiar forms are from Sagittarius and Pisces. Advachiel and Amnixiel by these figures.

```
    ★     ★                          ★
       ★                          ★     ★
    ★     ★      Acquisitio        ★     ★      Laetitia
       ★                          ★     ★
```

A King with a sword drawn riding on a Stag
A man wearing a Mitre in long raiment
A maid with a Laurel Crown adorned with flowers
A Bull
A Stag
A Peacock
An Azure garment
A Sword
A Box tree

After this manner do superior and inferior powers communicate.

THE THIRD OLYMPIC SPIRIT
MARS — PHALEG

Phaleg ruleth 35 visible Provinces. Phaleg ruleth those things attributed to Mars. He that have his Character he raiseth to great honour in warlike affairs.

The Spirits of Mars appear in a tall body, choleric, a filthy countenance, of colour brown, swarthy, or red having horns like hart's horns and griffin's claws bellowing like wild bulls. Their motion is like fire burning. Their sign is thunder and lightning about the Circle.

Particular forms:
    A King armed riding upon a wolf
    A man armed
    A woman holding a buckler on her thigh
    A he goat
    A horse
    A stag
    A red garment
    Wool
    Cheeslip [sic]

THE FOURTH OLYMPIC SPIRIT
THE SUN — OCH

Och governeth Solar things, he governeth 600 years with perfect health; he bestoweth great wisdom, giveth the most excellent spirits, teacheth perfect medicines. He converteth all things into most pure Gold and precious stones. He giveth Gold and a purse springing with Gold. He that is dignified with his Character he maketh him to be worshipped as a Deity by the Kings of the whole world.

He hath under him 36536 Legions. He administrates all things alone, and all his spirits serve him by centuries.

In Geomancy the Sun, or Sorath

★ ★		★	
★ ★	Fortuna	★	Fortuna
★	Major	★ ★	Minor
★		★ ★	

Shapes familiar to the Spirits of the Sun

The Spirits of the Sun do for the most part appear in a large full and great body, sanguine and gross in a gold colour with the tincture of blood.

Their motion is as the lightning of heaven, their sign is to move the person to sweat who calls them.

Their particular forms are:

A King having a Sceptre riding on a lion

A King crowned

A Queen with a sceptre

A bird

A lion

A cock

A yellow or golden garment

A sceptre

THE FIFTH OLYMPIC SPIRIT
VENUS — HAGGITH

Haggith governeth venereal things. He that is dignified with his Character he maketh very fair and to be adorned with all beauty. He converteth Copper into Gold in a moment, and Gold into Copper. He giveth spirits which do faithfully serve those to whom they are familiar. He hath 4000 legions of spirits and over every thousand he ordaineth Kings for their appointed seasons.

Kedemel	Kedemel
Hasmodel	Zuriel
♀ in ♉	♀ in ♎

Familiar shapes to the spirits of Venus

They appear with a fair body of middle stature with an amiable and pleasant countenance, of colour white or green, the upper part golden, the motion of them is as it were a most clear star. For their sign there will seem to be maids playing without the Circle which will provoke and allure him that calleth them to play.

Their particular forms are:
>   A King with a sceptre riding upon a camel
>   A maid clothed and dressed beautifully
>   A maid naked
>   A she goat
>   A camel
>   A dove
>   A white or green garment
>   Flowers
>   The herb savin

THE SIXTH OLYMPIC SPIRIT
MERCURY — OPHIEL

Ophiel is the Governor of such things as are attributed to Mercury. His spirits are 100,000 Legions. He easily giveth familiar spirits. He teacheth all arts and he that is dignified with his Character he maketh him to be able in a moment to convert Quicksilver into the Philosopher's Stone.

```
  ★   ★              ★   ★
  ★   ★              ★
    ★      Albus      ★          Conjunctio
  ★   ★              ★   ★
```

The Familiar forms of the Spirits of Mercury

The spirits of Mercury will appear for the most part in a body of middle stature, cold, liquid and moist, fair and with an affable speech in a human shape and form, like unto a Knight armed, of colour clear and bright. The motion of them is as it were silver coloured clouds. For their sign they bring horror and fear unto him that calls them.

The particular shapes are:

    A King riding upon a Bear
    A fair youth
    A woman holding a distaff
    A dog
    A she bear
    A Magpie
    A garment of sundry changeable colours
    A rod
    A little staff

THE SEVENTH OLYMPIC SPIRIT
THE MOON — PHUL

Phul changeth all metals into Silver in word and deed, governeth Lunary things, healeth the dropsy, he giveth spirits of the water who do serve men in a corporeal visible form and maketh men to live 300 years if God permit.

```
*   *                        *
*   *                        *
*   *   Populus              *   Via
*   *                        *
```

The forms familiar to the Spirits of the Moon

They will for the most part appear in a great and full body, soft and phlegmatic of colour, like a black obscure cloud, having a swelling countenance with eyes red and full of water, a bald head and teeth like a wild boar. Their motion is as it were an exceeding great tempest of the sea. For their sign there will appear an exceeding great rain about the Circle.

Their particular shapes are:

    A King like an Arthur riding on a Doe
    A little boy
    A woman hunter with a bow and arrows
    A cow
    A little doe
    A goose
    A garment green or silver coloured
    An arrow
    A creature having many feet

PHANES PRESS both publishes and distributes many fine books which relate to the philosophical, religious and spiritual traditions of the Western world. To obtain a copy of our current catalogue, please write:

PHANES PRESS
PO BOX 6114
GRAND RAPIDS, MI 49516
USA